Lost Restaurants of Henderson Nevada

Lost Restaurants of Henderson Nevada

SHARON ANN DAMON

Foreword by James Smerek

AMERICAN PALATE

Published by American Palate
A Division of The History Press
Charleston, SC
www.historypress.com

First published 2019

Manufactured in the United States

ISBN 9781467139373

Library of Congress Control Number: 2018963635

Notice: The information in this book is true and complete to the best of our knowledge. It is offered without guarantee on the part of the author or The History Press. The author and The History Press disclaim all liability in connection with the use of this book.

Dedicated to my greatest supporters: my mom, Alice Schellenberg, and my husband, Mike Damon.

To Mo, Laurie, Caly, Charlie and Izzy:

"You can do anything you set your mind to!"

xoxo Nana

Contents

Foreword

In 1996, the City of Henderson adopted the slogan "Henderson: A Place to Call Home" from entries submitted into a contest. For many Henderson residents, that's exactly what it is. For some of us, Henderson has been our only home.

I am second-generation "Henderson born." My grandfather, Paul Coroneos, moved to what is now Henderson with his parents and brothers in the early 1940s. It was not until 1953 that Henderson became incorporated into a small city, then with a population under ten thousand. My grandmother Marika Coroneos moved to Henderson in 1959 from Greece and was proud to become an American citizen soon after. My other grandparents, John and Dorothy Smerek, moved to Henderson from Michigan in the 1960s along with my dad and his siblings.

My sister and I were born in the same hospital as our mom, St. Rose De Lima—my mom in the original hospital, my sister and I in subsequent additions to the hospital. St. Rose has expanded considerably over the years and now includes other campuses and clinics across Henderson. My grandpa would tell us the story of how he worked on an addition for the Dominican sisters' quarters that still stands today, although it is used as offices along with the original wing of the hospital.

Over the years, I can't tell you how many times we were involved in what was then called the "Industrial Days" and its parade down Water Street. Industrial Days celebrated Henderson's World War II industrial roots, and the massive BMI Complex and its surrounding area continue to be a part of the city to this day. The tradition and parade live on today as "Heritage Days." I can still recall walking (later marching) the parade route many times, from the Gordon McCaw Elementary Kazoo Band, cub scouts, Burkholder Middle School Band and, lastly, the Foothill High School Marching Band. Heritage Days brings longtime and new Henderson residents alike together to celebrate the festivities and is fun for the whole family.

I started high school in 1999, the year Foothill High School opened. I would have been the third generation to attend Basic High School but instead was part of a new Henderson tradition. When Foothill opened, it split what is frequently known as "Old Henderson" in two. As a member of the marching band, I can still remember the first football game between the two schools, held at Basic. The stands on both sides of the field were full, and a standing crowd circled the field. This rivalry is now frequently referred to as the "Battle for Boulder Highway," a nod to Boulder Highway, which predates Henderson and serves largely as the dividing line between the school zones. The Foothill Marching Band is now the largest band in the state of Nevada and has received numerous local, national and even international recognition and awards. The band has marched in some of the most famous and prestigious parades in the world, including the St. Patrick's Day Parade in Dublin, Ireland; the Macy's Thanksgiving Day Parade in New York City; and, most recently, the Tournament of Roses Parade in Pasadena, California.

In recent years, downtown Henderson, now known as the "Water Street District," has seen a significant transformation. In addition to Heritage Days, Water Street hosts numerous art shows, car shows, conventions, a farmers' market and other events. I am proud that while this area is redeveloped, it holds true to its place as the traditional and cultural center of the city.

Henderson is now home to more than 300,000 people, according to recent U.S. Census estimates, and the city continues to grow. Henderson boosts many world-class amenities and master planned communities and has some of the best parks in the nation.

I am proud to continue to live in Henderson. The future certainly keeps looking bright for this city. For those of us among the longtime or native residents, as well as those who have more recently moved to the city, Henderson is a place we can all call home!

JAMES "JIMMY" SMEREK
Master of Education, Curriculum and Instruction, UNLV

Acknowledgements

It may take a village to raise a child, but it takes a community and network of friends, acquaintances and neighbors to write a book. With all the gratitude in my heart, I would like to thank the following individuals.

My husband, Mike Damon, researcher and history buff extraordinaire, spent endless hours helping me find photos and information about defunct places—not only in Henderson but also on our journeys throughout the state of Nevada. He kept me grounded when I took flights of fancy. Jimmy Smerek has been a great friend and CCSD teacher who possesses a knowledge of his lifelong home, Henderson, and the surrounding area that boggles the mind. I will be forever grateful (and thanks for the foreword!). My acquisitions editor, Laurie, patiently helped throughout the photo selection, layout and presentation processes—you were a constant support. I literally couldn't have done it without you! Also thanks to The History Press for taking a chance on my ability and for giving me the opportunity toward which I have been working for more than half my life. I owe a debt of thanks to Dana Bullinger (digital projects librarian for Henderson Libraries) and Colleen O'Brien (City of Henderson, City Clerk's Office) for their diligent assistance with sources and permission for use of the photos contained in this book. Ms. Bullinger was especially invaluable in the hunt for copies of photos. The Henderson Public Library/City of Henderson digital archives were a real blessing, providing photos that we otherwise would never have found, as was the *Review Journal*.

I'd be remiss if I didn't acknowledge my mom-in-law (and second mom), Jackie Damon—a photographer of epic proportions—for her knowledgeable encouragement, as well as my good friends Krista Demenezes, Joe Garcia, Donna Sunshine Caldwell and Sasha Illic for their suggestions of defunct places they recall from growing up as lifelong residents of Henderson. Many thanks to my "Nextdoor" and "You Know You're from Henderson if…" communities.

Many Facebook neighbors shared so many place names and experiences: Joyce Nunes (a fount of information), Toni (Ron) Oliverra (thank you for sharing your wonderful memories of the Gold Mine Tavern and your recipe for the Motherlode sandwich), Grace Slater (who even offered a book signing opportunity before the book was published), Paula Harris, Tia Martin, Dinah Wells Epp, Barbara Snearly, Darren Boggs, Michael Holland, Scott Elliot, Kathleen Congleton, Julie Graham, Sheila Parise, Ron Averett, Robin Apostalo, Ray Wilke, Casey Jade, Lisa Pitts, Stephan Crews, Phyllis LeFrancoise, Sandy Levitt, Heather Kelley, Claire Greenhaigh, Jane Martin Kennedy, James Cameron, Melissa Smith-Miller, Bruce Bainbridge, Brenda Toiya, David Duval, Sharon Hemmeter, John Nicholas (and his memories of Pappy Swift), Patsy Ackerman, Heather Eilene Carducci Kelley, Mary Arkell and so many more who gave tips and photos anonymously.

If I have omitted anyone or misspelled your name, it's my fault and I can only say "thank you so very much." My dearest friend, Yvonne Cutting, encouraged me throughout our forty-five-year friendship, before she passed away, to "go for it with gusto." She will always be my inspiration and role model. I especially owe my parents, Edward and Alice Lydia Schellenberg, an everlasting debt of gratitude for encouraging my attempts at "scribble-scrabbling" since I first picked up a pencil.

"Look, Ma, we did it!"

Introduction

While Las Vegas crowds the Valley, Henderson reaches for the mountaintops and water. Old topographical and survey maps created throughout the decades make this evident. Standing free from the glitz of the Strip to become its own entity—the second-largest city in Nevada—this sprawling city inspires pride and a sense of history in its residents. As its other motto states, "Henderson: A Great Place to Live." To understand the enduring grit and determination of those dwelling in this city, you have to comprehend the beginning of Las Vegas itself.

THE BEGINNING

In the early 1800s, Spanish explorers moved through Nevada, using this region as their waystation ever westward and south toward California in their search for land and the missions or colonies awaiting them. The Southern Paiute people traditionally made their homes in the area of the Southern California River and the Mojave Desert. In 1855, this area was annexed to the United States, and more settlers moved in, crowding the previously open territory and displacing many native residents. Mormon missionaries built a fort in 1855 in the Las Vegas Creek area fed by Big Springs (now Springs Preserve) before continuing their own journey westward. The area became hugely popular in the eastern part of the United States, and settlers thronged

Pittman, Nevada, aerial view, 1941. How this has changed throughout the years. *Courtesy of the Henderson Library Digital Collection (HLDC).*

to this new, exciting region, encouraged by a report written by John Frémont and Kit Carson promoting the Springs to readers. The passel of people staked claims for their homesteads, taking even more of the indigenous people's land. When pioneer rancher Helen J. Stewart realized that the Paiute culture was in danger, she gave them ten acres of Las Vegas Rancho in 1911, thus creating Las Vegas Indian Colony (the modern-day Las Vegas Paiute tribe simply refers to this plot of land, now thirty-one acres in size, as "The Colony"). William (W.A.) Clark was instrumental in bringing in the railroad and purchased land from Helen Stewart in 1902. He auctioned out parcels or lots to create a township in 1905. The ranch continued to operate until the early 1920s, and when Helen Stewart died in 1926, she was well-respected as the "First Lady of Las Vegas."

When Las Vegas and Henderson separated from Arizona territory to become part of Nevada in 1877, small farming communities developed in the desert and ranches were established, but the boom really began with the building of the Hoover Dam in 1931. At least twenty-one thousand workers swarmed into the area to work. Little tent camps (often called "Hootervilles") such as Railroad Pass, Texas Acres and Oklahoma City sprang up in the '30s to accommodate more workers. Las Vegas was unable to cope with the surge—they simply didn't have enough homes or developed space at the time and the city wasn't as close in proximity to the dam as Henderson. Jericho Heights, also known as Pittman—bounded by what today is Sunset Road to the north, Moser Street to the east, Merlayne Street to the south and Ward Drive to the west—housed some of these workers. In this way, just a handful of residents—mostly Native Americans, ranchers, farmers or dam workers—occupied this area of Nevada until the U.S. government established its magnesium plant in 1941 as part of the war effort and Pittman Camp was born almost overnight.

Chapter 1

Camp Pittman and BMI

War Needs, Magnesium and a Dream

In 1941, Howard Eells and his new company, Basic Magnesium Inc. (BMI), signed a contract with the U.S. Defense Plant Corporation to establish the Basic Magnesium Plant. This company was a joint venture between Magnesium Elektron Limited of England and Basic Refractories (a Cleveland, Ohio company of which Eells was the head). Magnesium was the lightest and strongest of metals, and separating the metal from its ore by electrolysis was vital to the war efforts because of its use in strengthening aluminum for the production of munitions and airplane parts. German pilots took advantage of the lighter construction of their dive bombers, which used magnesium parts, while their paratroopers could carry their own lightweight artillery constructed of the same material; manufacturers used it in the production of flares, tracer bullets and incendiary bombs.

The U.S. Army needed to catch up and ordered the construction of the plant to be at least 250 miles inland from the Pacific Ocean for the sake of national security. Las Vegas in 1941 was a tiny railroad watering station that was just starting to blossom with the building of casinos such as the El Rancho and El Cortez. What is now Henderson was simply empty land with a few scattered farms and ranches. The threat of war and the vast amount of available land such as this—with relative proximity to Lake Mead for water, the Hoover Dam for power and the mining claim named Brucite in Gabbs, Nevada (which was owned by Basic Refractories), for its deposits of magnesite—helped seal the selection of the Henderson area in plans to quickly develop the five-thousand-acre

Aerial view of BMI Townsite and Plant, 1941, which shows the sprawl and size of this endeavor. *Courtesy of the Henderson Library Digital Collection (HLDC).*

BMI site, which was slated to be constructed on what was previously wild land in this barren desert.

The plant was to be owned by the federal government, with day-to-day operations managed by BMI. Days after the contract was signed, the projected scale of the venture was expanded to ten times the original size—a mind-boggling 1.75 miles long and 0.75 mile wide—establishing Basic Magnesium as the largest magnesium plant in the world. Boulder City and Las Vegas simply were unprepared to house the more than thirteen thousand newly arrived workers, so they subsequently lived in ramshackle "tent cities" (Pittman Camp) due to their sheer numbers until Midway City—essentially a company town with amenities—was built in 1942. This was not in Eell's plans. It has been said that he didn't want anything to do with company towns, but it was necessary in order to comply with U.S. Public Housing Health Standard requirements to meet government specifications. BMI also constructed a railroad for transportation of raw magnesium from Gabbs,

350 miles northwest of the Henderson site, and a line from Henderson to the Union Pacific branch line in Boulder City, Nevada. Eventually, Washington built a new cost-efficient road connection (including a Las Vegas thoroughfare called Rancho Drive) to keep heavy trucks from tearing up the more fragile existing city roads. It is estimated that 25 percent of the power from the new Hoover Dam supplied the needs of the company and that power lines were run specifically to Pittman camp and BMI to fulfill their requirements. As the community grew, so did the draw on the power supply.

After Eells was investigated by Senator Harry Truman, chairman of the Senate Investigation Committee (at the urging of Las Vegas senator Berkeley Bunker), Eells was accused of using his plans to profit from the war effort. In 1942, he sold BMI to Anaconda Copper Mining Company. Anaconda completed the work on the town site and was responsible for bringing the plant to full production. The growing city was soon renamed after Charles B. Henderson, the former senator who helped in the initial push to get

Aerial view of Pittman Tent City grounds, 1942. Housing the many workers obviously took top priority as the BMI plant was constructed. *Courtesy of the Henderson Library Digital Collection (HLDC).*

the plant financed and built. Thus Henderson, the second-largest city in Nevada, was born.

For the next few years, BMI exceeded production rates, employing fourteen thousand employees at its peak. It was a bustling place with job opportunities galore, and as at Boulder Dam during its construction, the plant suffered considerable turnover due to the living conditions and the extreme heat. This was a huge spread on which to house the majority of workers. With families came their children. Necessities such as telegraph wires, power lines, stores, churches, a hospital, daycares and schools were quickly built for the needs of the many residents. Railroad Pass High School (renamed Basic High School three years later) was the first school to open. It was soon determined that families needed more space and that communities had to be built to house the burgeoning numbers of residents.

In 1943, the 300-unit Victory Village was built across the highway from BMI. It comprised apartments, separate dormitories for men and for women and "social/commercial service buildings" for the needs of lower-income white workers and their families. For the first

Ground view of Pittman Tent City living accommodations, 1942. This clearly shows the day-to-day living conditions of the workers. *Courtesy of the Henderson Library Digital Collection (HLDC).*

The original bombshell, Magnesium Maggie, hard at work at the BMI plant, 1942. Roll over, Rosie the Riveter! *Courtesy of the Henderson Library Digital Collection (HLDC).*

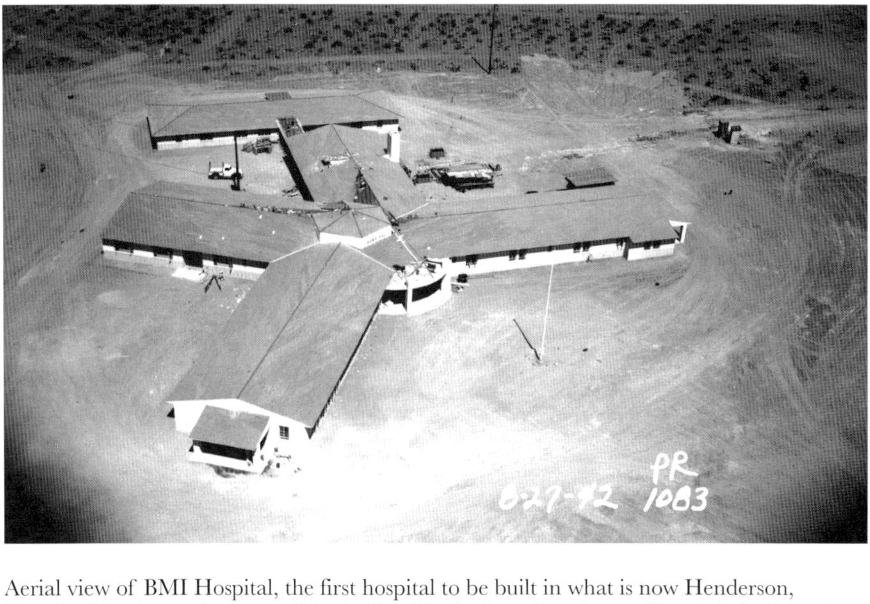

Aerial view of BMI Hospital, the first hospital to be built in what is now Henderson, Nevada. This is now known as Dignity Health: St. Rose Dominican Hospital, St. Rose de Lima Campus. *Courtesy of the Henderson Library Digital Collection (HLDC).*

Jane Fleming holding her son, Stephen, on Magnesium Street, 1942, in the Victory Village community. *Courtesy of Henderson Public Library, used with permission.*

The Williams family—Robert, Rosie Lee, Yvonne, Clarice, Roscoe, Theodore and Cleopatra—were the first family to move into Carver Park, October 13, 1943. *Courtesy of the Henderson Library Digital Collection (HLDC).*

time, segregation raised its head in this part of the country, and it was determined that a 324-unit housing development known as Carver Park should be constructed just northeast of Victory Village for African American workers and their families. The community was designed by Paul R. Williams, a prominent African American architect, and was named for George Washington Carver, a black humanitarian and scientist. Despite the division of communities, all children attended the same school, even though Carver Park housed its own preschool and recreation facility. As previously mentioned, Railroad Pass High School opened in 1942 (renamed Basic High School in 1945), the first library (on Pacific Avenue) opened for business in 1943 and the post office soon followed in January 1944. The municipal pool opened the next year. Business flourished, and a chamber of commerce was organized in 1945. Families grew and prospered as homes were built, and they were able to move out of the tents and dormitories into their own places. One can only imagine the pride these families took in their dwellings, being able to once again enjoy home life and have the opportunity to eat dinner gathered around their own tables instead of in a communal mess hall.

GHOST TOWN OR THRIVING COMMUNITY?

By 1947, after the end of the war, vast amounts of magnesium were no longer necessary for defense, and the BMI plant was subsequently closed since a considerable stockpile had been accrued. More than half of the employees abruptly picked up and left Nevada in the search for new jobs and stable living conditions. Soon Henderson was under threat of becoming a ghost town, as so many of the city's former residents all but disappeared and homes and businesses were deserted. Schools lost about two-thirds of their students, and remaining businesses struggled to survive. Things looked bleak. In 1947, the U.S. War Asset Administration tried to sell the city as war-surplus property—highlighting the available housing, churches, shops, bowling alley, organized streets, schools, businesses and such assets.

On February 28, the Henderson and Las Vegas Chamber of Commerce offered Nevada legislators the opportunity to visit Southern Nevada and Henderson with the proposal that they would, in essence, purchase it. A few days after the visit, a bill was approved that permitted the Colorado River Commission of Nevada to act as the state's negotiator to buy Henderson and the magnesium plant since it was their responsibility to ensure Nevada's rights and interest in the Colorado River and in the electric power generated at Hoover Dam. Governor Vail Pittman signed the bill on March 27. The Henderson Chamber of Commerce had also convinced the Las Vegas Chamber of Commerce to invite the representatives from the Nevada legislature to visit Boulder (now Hoover) Dam to evaluate the BMI site and consider construction of a power generator at the dam to bring in new workers (i.e., residents) and provide employment for the remaining people still living here. Thankfully, it worked and Henderson was saved.

There were still many unused buildings and empty property available to be purchased or repurposed with the demise of BMI, including area businesses that were in a state of flux. Once Henderson was safe from sale, it was time to consider its future use. Industrial firms such as Chemstar Lime Inc., Kerr McGee Chemical Corporation, Pioneer Chlor Alkali Company and Timet used former BMI buildings to set up shop in what became known as the Basic Management Industrial Complex. By 1952, the tenth anniversary of the town site's founding, Henderson had begun to brand itself as "Nevada's Industrial Center," marking Henderson as a "city of industry," which had been our city's civic goal for more than forty years.

The 1949 Basic Township flood. Even with natural washes, Las Vegas and Henderson were both prone to severe flash floods, and this one was no exception. *City of Henderson Secure File (copy of original), used with permission.*

Midway housing, well and casino (1943). *Courtesy of the Henderson Library Digital Collection (HLDC).*

But sometimes progress needs a bit of ingenuity, thinking outside the box or "knowing someone who knew someone" to get things done. After receiving a letter from Father Peter Moran, pastor of St. Peter's Church in Henderson, suggesting that the Adrian Dominican Sisters of Michigan might want to consider purchasing the city's first hospital, the Sisters agreed to the venture. In order to meet public need, the government gave them BMI Hospital in 1947, and the Sisters renamed it Rose de Lima. It has since been renamed, first as St. Rose Dominican Hospital, which is still in use to this day at 102 East Lake Mead Parkway, and then its most current title of Dignity Health: St. Rose Dominican Hospital, St. Rose de Lima Campus.

THE BIRTH OF A CITY

In 1953, Henderson's incorporation degree was issued for its original thirteen-square-mile stretch including Pittman, the original Basic Townsite

BMI Day Nursery is one of the amenities built for families at the Townsite, circa 1942. *Courtesy of the Henderson Library Digital Collection (HLDC).*

(bounded by Boulder Highway, Lake Mead Drive, Victory Avenue, Van Wagenan Street, Tin Street and Ocean Avenue). Dr. J.B. French was elected the first city mayor on May 23. The population was estimated at about 7,500 residents at this time. The first recreation center was built in 1956, courtesy of a fundraising concert featuring celebrities like Frank Sinatra, and a number of parks were added, starting the growth of our celebrated green space. On July 23, 1963, President John F. Kennedy signed the Henderson Land Bill, doubling the size of the city by adding fifteen thousand acres of land to the township, mostly to the west of Henderson's original property lines. This, of course, opened the door to future expansion.

The BMI Pool and Recreation Center

There were several places built in the 1940s that were still every bit as popular in the '50s, '60s and beyond—some lasting even to this day. Many lifelong residents remember the BMI Pool and Recreation Center, where they would spend hours keeping safe and off the streets, staying cool in the pool and hanging out playing games and socializing with their friends. Claire Greenhalgh recalled that "the rec center had pool tables, basketball hoops and they held team games and once a month they would have movies for the kids and it only cost a quarter." Jane Martin Kennedy added, "There was a stage [as James Cameron recalled "at the south end of the basketball court"]. In the '60s we had dances there on Friday and Saturday nights, and the bands would play on that stage! They were local groups, but always so good as I remember!" Bruce Bainbridge went there in the '70s to play Wiffle ball, pool, swim, play basketball and ping-pong for hours. David Duval also remembered the Wiffle ball and added that "at Thanksgiving time they had a turkey shoot with real BB guns and you got to bring home a turkey if you won." John Nicholas will never forget that Pappy Swift lived on Ocean. "He worked at the Rec Center. Taught a lot of us to shoot pool and snooker. He was over seventy in the late '60s. He always had an ear for the teens there, didn't matter who you were." That was the whole point—everyone felt welcome here!

Melissa Smith-Miller also had many fond memories of her own to share:

> *I attended the BMI rec center in the late '80s and early '90s every single summer until…well, honestly, I don't know, it seems forever. Both my parents were working full time, and my mother would sign me and my brother up for the summer magic program, which was pretty much like a daycare for kids. It was a big red brick building, and when you walked in, it had a solid wood gym floor. (And I believe a stage at the end of the gym.) And correct me if I'm wrong, they had two rooms that were off to the left that had pool tables, foosball tables, TV and vending machines with all kinds of munchies and candy. And then when you looked to the left, there was like the metal mesh teal blue glass window protector that covered the whole glass window. That was the patio kids went out and hung on. Then through the back of the patio and out some double gates you would walk next door to the set of three pools and swim all day. Sometimes the program would take us on fieldtrips, arts and crafts days, movie and swimming day. The first pool being the kiddie pool, then the big one that was the main pool and then the diving one. I look back now and get choked up, and I'm truly grateful that I have these memories. I will always hold them dear to my heart, as I think these years of my childhood honestly were the happiest and the best years of my life.*

James Cameron kindly shared a photo and noted, "This is an early picture of the youth center on the left and BMI pool entrance on the right. The parking lot was yet to be paved." I wish we could have used it but it was definitely representative of Henderson's growth and development.

The pool has recently been "extensively" renovated and stands beside Downtown Park and the Downtown Rec Center, even after all these years. You can still take swimming lessons or open swim at this outdoor pool. It now features a diving tank, lap lanes, a kiddie pool and an eight-foot tall AquaClimb climbing wall! The pool is still only open during the summer, as always.

BASIC HIGH SCHOOL

Lifelong local, Henderson expert and Basic High School graduate Jimmy Smerek shared this information about his school:

> *The 1954 Basic High School Gym at Burkholder Middle School is one of the oldest school buildings in Clark County. When Basic High School opened in the 1940s, it was located where city hall and the police department now stand on Basic Road. Nothing remains of the original school. The school moved to the Van Wagenan site in 1954,*

Basic High School, the first school to be built in what is now Henderson, Nevada. Today, only a plaque on the gym wall shows that it once existed. *City of Henderson Secure File (copy of original), used with permission, photo #0033.*

and the junior high school took the place of the old school. In 1973, the school moved to its current location. The Van Wagenan School became "Burkholder Junior High" (now Burkholder Middle School). The gym was damaged when it survived the PEPCON blast of 1988 and a fire in the early '90s. When they tore down the old campus to build the current Burkholder Middle school (after the old school closed in 2004), they saved the gym. This is the only remaining original 1954 structure still at the site. The old gym is now the activity center/cafeteria for the new school, having been replaced by a new gymnasium. A plaque still reads "Basic High School Gymnasium, Erected 1954" on the front of the old gym. Basic was one of the first four high schools as the Valley grew: Las Vegas, Boulder City, Basic (Henderson) and Rancho (North Las Vegas). Basic Elementary School was later renamed Gordon McCaw Elementary School and has operated since 1953, although the original building was replaced in 2009.

Henderson continued to slowly grow throughout the 1960s and 1970s, thriving as a small factory town. The city spread and developed, proving Kennedy's vision for Henderson as a "city of destiny" to be true. Businesses flourished in the name of progress. The influx of new residents looking for opportunities provided the need for more churches in a variety of denominations and for additional schools to be built in order to accommodate the growing city population. Work was steady, life was relatively calm, families continued to grow and more homes were, in turn, built to house them as businesses prospered. Henderson was beginning to boom by the end of the '70s.

In the early 1980s, Green Valley—4,800 acres in the southeast part of the Las Vegas Valley—was established as the first master-planned community in Henderson. But then, on May 4, 1988, tragedy hit as Henderson was shaken by the explosion of the Pacific Engineering and Production Company of Nevada (PEPCON). The rocket fuel factory caught fire and caused several explosions that measured 3.0 on the Richter scale. People living miles away felt the blast, as the explosion shattered windows and shook buildings to their foundations, killing two and injuring three hundred people. The blast caused havoc, with firefighters rushing to contain the damage, blowing out the windshield of a fire engine and destroying the fire chief's car in the process (he and his driver luckily escaped with minor injuries). The explosions left a two-hundred-foot crater in their wake, and the nearby Kidd & Company

Marshmallow Factory also went up in flames. Schools and businesses in the vicinity had to be temporarily evacuated and closed for the sake of safety. This resulted in Henderson's transformation to a residential community from the originally envisioned industrial city. This is not to say, however, that industry completely halted in town—the focus simply changed as life went on.

Our town continued to spread until, in 1999, Henderson overtook Reno as the second-largest city in Nevada. In 2003, Henderson celebrated its fiftieth birthday with great fanfare, and there are no signs of our city's growth slowing any time in the near future. The population increase continues with the massive development of the Cadence master plan and other new housing projects, some of which sit on former BMI property, while others open up new territory, stretching up into the hillsides ever farther and into the realm of what was once barren desert. *Forbes* has twice promoted Henderson, rating it as one of the safest places to live and one of the top suburbs for retirement, as locals already realized. Accolades such as these helped open the eyes of people living throughout the country to the possibility of living in this city and has served as a great marketing tool to further help increase population to almost 300,000 residents at last count. The combination of temperate winters, accessibility to water and green spaces, natural wonders and employment opportunities, plus the boom in housing, makes our city attractive to people of all walks and stages of life.

The area surrounding Henderson has always boasted some of the most striking scenic sights to be found in Nevada—natural and man-made. It is not all desert! The stately mountain formations of nearby Mount Charleston, with its snow-capped peaks; the sheer beauty of Red Rock Canyon; the vivid colors of Valley of Fire at sunrise and sunset; a variety of hiking trails (including Railroad Pass); and the large parks that have been established for families (and pets) living in various communities are in stark contrast to the desert itself. Attractions such as Lake Las Vegas and the Wetlands Park and bird sanctuary attest to the wealth of variety in the Henderson area, as they provide shelter and roosting nests for the birds that live here all year long or migrate here twice a year. Hoover Dam brings with it a sense of history and wonder in human ingenuity and backbreaking labor. Lake Mead, with its recreation area and the waterways and campgrounds, plus the large number of vast planned green spaces scattered throughout Henderson, makes this one of the most beautiful places to live. It is a true oasis in the desert.

The BMI Dining Hall was an escape from the overwhelming desert heat in the summer and the chill winds in the winter. Families gathered communally to enjoy simple, hearty fare designed to give energy to the crews and their families living in the tent cities. *Courtesy of the Henderson Library Digital Collection (HLDC).*

Many locals of a wide variety of ages, nationalities and cultures have now lived here for two or more generations, while others were born here. Newcomers to our city are simply happy to take up residence in the proximity of (but not within) the more hectic city of Las Vegas. Henderson's location is also convenient for commuters. But all this attests to the fact that this city is far more than a simple satellite bedroom community. It is home, and as such, residents are proud of their history and accomplishments. Over the years, so many popular, unique businesses have opened and closed—restaurants included—but while Las Vegas looks to the future by often imploding and sometimes even burying the past, Henderson celebrates bygone days by keeping its history alive with online groups, preservation and historical societies' restoration projects and the efforts to showcase the area's history with displays of everyday life throughout the decades, as undertaken by the Clark County Museum reusing and recycling found spaces. This seems to be part of the Henderson way of life.

Defunct "lost" restaurants are fondly recalled by locals and tourists alike. They remember, they reminisce, families share stories and photos while friends tell each other of bygone days. Locals are always willing to share with guests, educating them and pointing out places of interest—but most of all making them feel welcome. This is the spirit of this book: to look forward by celebrating and recalling establishments that have played such a great part in the lives of locals and are still held within our hearts, as well as to acknowledge the places that have somehow withstood the test of time.

Chapter 2

The Need to Feed the Masses

The First Eateries

Since the days of the Old West, folks have sought out places to "sit a spell" and enjoy some liquid libation and a good meal or congenial company with spirited conversation. Whether the area housed farmers, cowboys, ranchers or settlers, this has also been the case throughout this region of the nation. But life in the desert brings its own challenges not found elsewhere: unrelenting heat for four or five months of the year, drought conditions with sparse rain or snow, sudden high winds and severe weather conditions including dust storms and flash floods. The challenge of the struggle to survive can only be imagined in the days before air conditioning and other creature comforts. When you combine the backbreaking work and challenge of building the indomitable Hoover Dam followed soon after by the frenetic rush to assemble a gigantic magnesium plant from the ground up to assist the war effort, you have a huge number of hungry workers to feed. Some sought out available small bars, coffee shops and diners, while others with families preferred a good home-cooked meal (or the closest thing they could get to that). While you lived in a tent city such as Pittman, you would pretty much have to eat in a massive communal mess hall or dining tent such as that created by BMI for its workers. This meant sitting elbow to elbow with other families at long tables, enjoying mass-produced food that was basic, stick-to-your ribs fare designed to give you the energy you needed to keep on going, day after day.

There were some amenities, even a small casino in Pittman (of course there was—this is Nevada after all), where you could gamble away a portion of your hard-earned cash while following the American Dream. There was a store for basic needs, a pharmacy, bars, a community well, a small hospital, a church, a school, a daycare and more. But the workers naturally wanted to socialize and spend time with friends and coworkers, and that meant getting all dolled up to go out on the town occasionally. Those who worked together played together, as group events were often planned for the enjoyment of all the residents living there. This might have included a community dance, party or other event held by residents and/or management to keep workers and their families happy by breaking up the day-to-day monotony, giving them something exciting to look forward to. Activities like holiday parties, Christmas and Halloween dances and other special events created a bond and resulted in lifelong friendships between many workers. Often these parties were themed, much to the delight of all the participants.

Once Henderson was established in 1953, many local families, just like today, wanted to go out for a sit-down meal, catch a snack or just escape for a short while. It was a novel treat to get out of the house and have a chance to socialize with others outside your own living or dining room. This was also an opportunity for the family to sit down, talk about their days and enjoy one another's company without interruption and meal preparation. Let's face it, Mom enjoyed being able to relax too! This was the era when the area eateries and bars began to grow in variety and number and thrived. Business boomed, and your number of alternatives ranged from casinos to bars, snack bars, diners, small restaurants or fine larger establishments such as the Swanky Club.

The Swanky Club

When there was nothing but desert around and the only road to get you from here to there was Boulder Highway, the Swanky Club (referred to by some as "Frankie Carr's Swanky Club") was a popular roadside attraction that has been likened to an oasis in an area still teeming with desert tortoises and other creatures. It was located at 920 North Boulder Highway in Pittman, aka Henderson. A trip to Henderson was a trip to "town" and one not taken lightly. In those days, "swanky" meant flashy,

Activities such as this barn dance at the BMI Campsite were very popular with the workers as a way to have fun with friends and coworkers while blowing off some steam. *Courtesy of the Henderson Library Digital Collection (HLDC).*

The venerable Swanky Club was the forerunner to many current buffets with its "all you can eat Smorgasbord," complete with communal tables, attentive service and crowds of hungry patrons. It is fondly remembered by many as a true "swanky" experience. *Courtesy of the Henderson Library Digital Collection (HLDC).*

luxurious, stylish and expensive, and according to longtime residents, this was a cool place with a great "vibe." There were long tables with tablecloths and candles on them and rather plain decorations on the walls, but the "all you can eat" food was what patrons enjoyed most. Its Wednesday night slow-roasted spare ribs were legendary, with or without barbecue sauce, as many attested. Another local shared that "I learned to love pickled pig's feet at the Swanky Club. Mom and Dad would stop there on their way to games as it really was the only restaurant for several miles."

Folks arrived all dressed up to enjoy "dining out," sometimes with entertainment (including "Phyllis Dilly," who, as one guest remembered, played the piano or organ on the weekends to keep diners entertained). The interior was nothing special—photos show (and folks remember) long, close-set communal tables with tablecloths and plain folding chairs for guests to sit on; the photos also show that it was a bit crowded. The kitchen was near the front entrance for at least part of its run, as a friend recalled, but the servers managed to get around to retrieve plates and refill glasses. Modest seasonal decorations helped to somewhat liven up the joint, but the whole Smorgasbord (aka "all you can eat") deal with service was a real treat since it meant Mom didn't have to do her usual dinner preparation or cleanup and families could enjoy a variety of fare other than their normal in a lively atmosphere. What a novelty for the residents who lived in the area! This was the forerunner to modern casino or other establishment's buffets and was still something new in those days. The Swanky Club also apparently catered area special events and functions, which was great for business. (As an aside, according to sources, the Swanky Club was owned by Jack and his wife, Doris Mallory, parents of John Mallory, the first Korean War veteran killed in action, just before his twentieth birthday. Mallory Street was named in his honor.)

LEGIONS, BARS AND COFFEE SHOPS

Veterans joined organizations such as the American Legion, where they and their families could enjoy tasty eats combined with amusing or toe-tapping entertainment on occasion. It may have been a bit crowded at the Legion, just as it was at the Swanky Club, but that was simply accepted as the way it was in those days. Visiting the Legion was a great

The American Legion has always been a place for veterans and their families to reminisce with friends, remember those who have passed and celebrate special events. *City of Henderson Secure Files (copy of original), used with permission.*

Establishments such as Dunc'n Shirley's Coffee Shop were the forerunner to many more mom and pop–style operations in Henderson. They were friendly, comfortable places for a snack or light meal. Shown are Ray Duncan (*left*) and Shirley Duncan. *City of Henderson Secure Files (copy of original), used with permission, photo #1142 HHN 7/24/58, p. 4.*

way to celebrate and reminisce with friends, to remember those who had passed and to plan events, as Legions still are to this day. Bars such as the Corral Bar in Pittman continued to be an alternative, as always, since it offered inexpensive drinks and bar food enjoyed by regular folks with the possibility of a game of pool or a card game. Then came the boom of the late '50s and '60s. As city growth increased, residents' desire for home cooking and comfort food rivaled what was offered at the casinos of the day and what was to be found at expensive larger establishments, so mom and pop establishments soon opened to the public. Places like Dunc'n Shirley's Coffee Shop were great for guests to grab breakfast before work or lunch on their breaks or while shopping, or they could enjoy a meal with coworkers or friends after the workday was done. Whether you worked in an office or on the road, you were always welcomed with a smile and a warm greeting (and the daily specials). Simple lunch bars like this paved the way for the more ambitious restaurants to come.

Chapter 3

Mom and Pop Stops

Once the '50s hit, most residents living in Henderson needed vehicles or were forced to rely on getting a ride with a coworker, walking long distances or using the iffy, off-and-on public transportation of the time (by all accounts). The town was gradually spreading out since its incorporation in 1953, and in order to get to work with population growth (more than 5,700 residents, according to the 1950 census), those who found employment often had to commute. This also meant eating on the run—catching a quick bite for breakfast, grabbing a hasty lunch or finally relaxing at a restaurant on the way home at the end of a long day. This was true for those who commuted greater distances, too, since it could very well be a long spell between breakfast, lunch and dinner. This is where the mom and pop establishments came into play—places where you always felt welcome and perhaps even like part of a bigger family. You felt at home and were likely to return time after time.

THE GOLD MINE TAVERN

Establishments like the Gold Mine Tavern at 23 South Water Street (which still survives with a new owner and a new style and format after having been closed for a while) thrived, offering a *Cheers*-like atmosphere to the daytime and after-work crowd, according to Toni Oliverra, wife of former owner

Ron Oliverra. She has many fond memories of helping run the deli and bar and of the faithful clients—friends who would visit almost daily to enjoy the food and the companionship, not to mention the drinks. It was a warm, congenial place. "There were two or three owners prior to Ron," shared Toni. She ran the deli while Ron ran the rest of the business from 1981 to 2007. Three generations of clients would bring their children in to celebrate their twenty-first birthdays with a first drink as part of the festivities, which many times included a visit to their place. The Gold Mine was dearly loved in this close-knit community. "If the girls went shopping, they would stop by to have a couple of drinks before going shopping again," Toni added. This was the second bar in the Valley to have karaoke on the stage in the middle of the place, and it was very popular, she proudly recalled.

The tavern was big enough to have at least five pool tables, where everyone from businessmen to bikers would try their skill while others enjoyed the karaoke or just relaxed, chatting at the bar. The music was mostly country-western, and the style was comfortable and laid-back. This establishment was so well-known and popular that the Gold Mine Tavern even garnered a spot on the Henderson Monopoly Game when it came out in 2016, as Toni shared. Their regulars were protective of the Oliverras—they truly cared for Toni and Ron's well-being. "If someone was '86'd' for behavior, Ron escorted them out kindly. He would turn them around and say, 'Look up,' and they did. 'Can you see the sign?' They would reply 'Yes,' and he would say, 'Don't ever walk under that sign again.'" Toni shared that sometimes those barred from the premises were devastated and had a bit of trouble taking no for an answer, so the other patrons made sure they complied with Ron and Toni's directions.

Toni also recalled her very popular and delicious "great Motherlode sandwiches in the Grubsteak Sandwich Shoppe" with obvious pride. The bread was specially proofed and baked by Smith's grocery store—the only place in the area willing to do this for them. Toni didn't come up with the recipe—the previous deli owner, Mary Kay, who ran the deli for two or three years prior to her had that honor—but "I do know what [this sandwich] was and how it was made since I owned the Deli/Sandwich shop that was inside the bar. We did deliveries, catered parties for many different organizations in town." Toni also took pride in the fact that she fashioned the clever bar menu, which was essentially a picture of the Motherlode sandwich that opened up to display the menu itself. Folks would come in to pick up the regular Motherlode—which was eighteen to nineteen inches long—to take out for a day on the lake, to enjoy at home with the family or to share at a picnic. It sold for six dollars at the time—remember, this was in the days before sub sandwich shops, so it was a real novelty! If you managed to eat one by yourself on premises, you could get a drink for free ("or perhaps even another sandwich," as Toni recalled). There was also a smaller version on the lunch menu and a humongous six-foot-long Motherlode on the catering menu. This was definitely *the* experience of its time, and it is clearly remembered by many native Henderson residents, as is the Gold Mine itself.

The Motherlode Sandwich

French bread (specially proofed and baked by Smiths)
5 meats (ham, beef, pastrami, turkey and salami)
2 cheeses (usually Swiss and provolone or cheddar)
mustard
mayonnaise

Load the ingredients up and enjoy the motherlode of all sandwiches.

THE VICTORY THEATER

Family-run businesses opened, providing employment for locals as well as the chance to own your own business, a dream shared by many. There were sometimes occasions when an establishment started out as something totally different and needed to be revamped to meet the proprietor's needs. All it took was a little ingenuity on the part of the owner. Almost everyone loved the idea of watching movies, so there was great excitement when the Victory Theater on or near Water Street opened its doors to sell-out crowds in February 1943 on what was the BMI township. The first movie shown was *Presenting Lily Mars* with Judy Garland. The theater gave residents a novel experience while expanding their worldview to consider more possibilities as they watched the news reels and feature films of the day. And let's face it—this was also great fun for the younger set!

The Victory was one of the most popular places for neighborhood kids to go on Saturday morning, and management occasionally hosted Boy Scout groups on certain days—as old photos show and patrons recall—for a rousing good time. Some believed that the business was started by BMI for the entertainment of its workers but it is now known to have actually been owned and operated by N.J. Van Wagenan. In 1954, he made Nevada history

The interior of the Victory Theater, BMI Townsite. It may have been plain compared to many present-day cinemas, but it had the biggest screen in this part of the country. *Courtesy of the Henderson Library Digital Collection (HLDC).*

The grand opening of the Victory Theater, BMI Townsite. It was *the* place to be on a Saturday morning. The crowds were waiting at the doors. *Courtesy of the Henderson Library Digital Collection (HLDC).*

by installing a twenty-one-by-forty-three-foot screen, the largest in the state. The Victory Theater was one-story and very utilitarian—almost like a hall in appearance rather than today's theaters—with rows of folding seats, aisles dividing the seating area on the left and right and steps leading up to the curtain-draped screen at the front of the theater. One can speculate that there must have been an upper floor specially designated for the projection booth. There were exits to the right and left of the screen, and you entered from the rear. The theater was apparently somewhat updated and remodeled as the years passed, but the basic format remained the same. A few residents recall that it was situated on a small street that was in between Navy and Panama, across from the fire department. "I can still remember being dropped off by the family station wagon for the Saturday cartoons and a show," reminisced one former patron. Another person remembered a snack bar with typical movie snacks near the entrance, but it was the experience that kept bringing in the movie lovers. The Victory Theater operated until 1989, when it was demolished. A parking lot for the Emerald Island Casino is now on the former site, but the memories still linger.

NICK'S SUPPER CLUB

Lifelong Henderson resident Jimmy Smerek fondly remembered his dad and grandfather (businessmen in their own right) sharing stories of downtown's Nick's Supper Club at 15 East Lake Mead Drive. This business was the reincarnation of Dante's Supper Club, according to other residents, and whenever asked, the fond memories came flooding in from everyone who had ever visited the place or those whose families had history to share. Jimmy's family knew the family who owned Nick's, frequented the restaurant and recalled how Nick came to Henderson from Greece (the "old country") in the 1960s for the opportunity to realize his dream and open his own establishment. Nick's offered excellent traditional Greek food (and a variety of other dishes) at fair cost to a very appreciative crowd.

Sasha Illic shared that "Nick's Supper Club was the place to go on Friday nights. I remember ordering Shirley Temples and feeling so grown up because the atmosphere was dark and semi-fancy feeling." Debra Avery remembered, "Nicks Supper Club had the best steak and lobster ever. Shrimp cocktail was huge and delicious. We would take our kids there for good report cards. They loved it!" Brenda Toiya's mother worked at Nick's

Supper Club/Dante's as a cocktail waitress for years. Her brother was also a dishwasher there. Nick's nephew, Evan Lathouris, was born and raised in Achladokampos, Greece, and at the age of eighteen, he followed Nick from the old country to legally immigrate to the United States, moving to Henderson to work at his uncle's restaurant from the ground up. It was here that he graduated from Basic High School, where he met his future wife, Vicki. Nick's Supper Club closed with Nick's passing in 1996, and extensive damage was caused to the empty building by a fire in May 2003. Evan soon went on to start his own place in Boulder City using the tools of the trade learned from his uncle, so in this sense, the legacy continues.

EVAN'S OLD TOWN GRILLE

Evangelos (Evan) and Vicki Lathouris have owned and operated their own tiny thriving business, Evan's Old Town Grille, since 1997. It is located at 1129 Arizona Street in the lovely historic district of Boulder City. This vibrant little establishment is charming, attractive and cozy, definitely "old school" in the best sense of the word, as we discovered. There is a small six-seater (or so), well-appointed bar near the entrance, with an excellent and very friendly bartender who has been working there for seventeen years, her "after-retirement" job. The restaurant boasts about ten to twelve tables—each holding a maximum of two to six patrons—well-spaced on the floor and to the side of the bar to allow for walking room. This is the place to visit to find some of the tastiest, most freshly prepared food around the Valley, and at reasonable cost. It gives the phrase "intimate dining" a whole new meaning.

According to Vicki—who is also the greeter—their establishment hosts guests from around the world, around the country and all over Nevada and California, as well as a steady base of staunch locals who appreciate great food. Reservations may be needed on busy evenings to avoid a wait, but if you don't have one, as we found, they do their best to seat you as soon as possible. Regulars meet here, travelers stop by on their way "to and from," families celebrate special occasions and campers enjoy it as a respite from their tents and RVs. As one elderly gentleman noted to Vicki at the door, "I'm just glad you're here." The specialty Greek salad is very tasty, tossed with Evan's special dressing, and the deboned grilled trout is the tastiest I have ever enjoyed. The chicken cordon bleu (sometimes on the daily special board) is excellent, as attested by my husband, Mike, and we both really enjoyed the fresh breadsticks. You can create your own pasta dishes, and the desserts—including baklava and tiramisu (and, of course, spumoni ice cream)—are pure decadence. Make sure to ask your friendly and efficient server about any drink specials and check the board for daily dining specials—they are well worth it. You never know what Evan is going to cook up next, and he even walks through the restaurant each evening to make sure all is well. This place is very accommodating about dietary-related requests, as related by some other diners. The whole experience is further proof that what Evan learned from his experience with his Uncle Nick obviously paid off. This place is bustling, and it's easy to see why.

Aurelio's Pizza Restaurant opened its doors at 10960 South Eastern Avenue in Henderson in 1959 as a family pizzeria. The atmosphere was casual, homey and comfortable, and the menu featured all your Italian favorites, including delicious varieties of thin- and thick-crust pizza and several pasta dishes, giving this part of town the chance to enjoy this relatively "new" and very popular favorite. The date of its closing seems to be in 2013, so the business had a good long run for a few generations to an appreciative audience. It is still missed by many residents, who remember the pizza from when they were young, and others miss the bosco sticks, karaoke and arcade games.

Joyce Nunes is the only person I spoke to who could share memories of the unique Buster's BBQ, "a mobile BBQ that was located in the Pittman neighborhood near Wells Park. They cooked all the time, and the neighborhood smelled so delicious. People could just walk up to their smoker and buy right from it in front of their house. They also traveled all over the valley with it and were well known." This was a unique service that was never duplicated and was obviously well known, well used and appreciated. She also recalled "the Villa Pizza by Cinedome 21 theater (now closed) [as being] a fixture on Greenway and Boulder—later Lake Mead and Boulder—for many years." Several lifelong residents mentioned this place in passing when discussing long-gone places. It was a neighborhood favorite.

The 1960s brought further growth, with plazas and stretches of businesses springing up the length of Boulder Highway and the Market area. Communities grew within the various pockets of land in the area. Victory Village expanded, and the area around Major Avenue blossomed as the population grew and the demand for more choice in services increased. The ride toward Boulder City suddenly didn't seem so long anymore, nor the road so endless, once the gravel stretch was eventually paved, and there were places you could stop at along the way to get a treat or supplies. Henderson had boomed from thirteen square miles at its inception to doubling in 1963 with the passing of the Henderson Land Bill. The population grew almost four times between 1950 and 1960, exceeding 12,500 residents. Growth emphasized the desire for variety and the opportunity for burgeoning entrepreneurs to take a risk and spread their culinary wings as more and more land became available for purchase or lease. For many, their dreams soon became reality.

There are several particular businesses near and dear to the hearts of those who were children or teens growing up in Henderson. Resident Joe Garcia couldn't pass up the opportunity to rave about Pac-Out Burgers as one of his childhood favorites. The year it was established is uncertain, but the memory of the cheese fries doused in sauce, as Joe shared, still lingers with residents, and this burger joint simply can't be ignored. Once reminded of this place, kudos came pouring in, making it a definite much-missed local haunt. There was even some friendly competition between various local businesses—the fast-food shops and drive-ins—especially those drawing in the considerable hungry teen lunch crowd. One local recalled that "Pac-Out was across from the Eldorado Casino while Arctic Circle was close to Lake Mead on Water. The hamburgers and shakes made them popular places for high school kids."

Downtown Henderson Market area stores including Foodland, Utility Service Light Gas Power and possibly the school, May 1, 1964. *City of Henderson Secure Files (copy of original), used with permission, photo #00047.*

Sharon Hemmeter fondly shared, "In the early '70s, when lunchtime came around, my friends and I would leave school [Basic] and drive to the Pac-Out for tacos and Dr Pepper. It was our best time ever because others from school would be there. We would blast our car radios and dance, have fun talking, laughing, and when it was time to go back, if we went back, we could eat our tacos on the way. Good memories."

Potrillo's was built on the Pac-Out lot after its demise but quickly closed within a few years, according to longtime residents frequenting the "You Know You're from Henderson if…" Facebook page. Potrillo's specialties were such culinary delights as the Steamie Weenie, Pink's Hot Dogs, Cheffini's Hot Dogs, Windy City Beefs N Pizza, Windy City Beefs N Dogs, Amore Taste of Chicago, Plantone's Italian, Cheffinis Hot Dogs—The Cart, American Coney Island Chili. Nothing fancy but some clever names, and the dogs were consistently tasty, according to reviews from several locals.

Sometimes a place stirs up notice in not-so-positive ways. Many neighbors have raved or complained, in turn, about China Joe's Restaurant at 720 South Boulder Highway and North Major Avenue. This was a conveniently located dining establishment that was very popular from the early 2000s until 2013, after which patrons said they were disappointed to see new management come in with different values and priorities and the ratings started to plummet. It was still a go-to place for many area residents because of its convenience until it closed in 2015. By then the place's reputation and subsequent popularity had apparently declined. A few locals, including Sasha Illic and our neighbor Bill, asked that it be included because of its decent cost and perfect location. Both Sasha and Bill agreed that "the food was pretty great, too." You can tell by the menu still posted on the glass that there was definitely no lack of variety. The name has also not yet been removed from the building, keeping the memory alive for those who used to enjoy it and now just pass it by.

Boulder Bowl (in Boulder City) and Henderson Bowling Alley were preferred hangouts for local teens and bowling enthusiasts. What better way to spend a hot summer day or winter evening than to visit with your teammates, go on a date, eat some fast food and throw a few balls down the lanes? When you live in the desert, sometimes retreating to a cool place to hang out is the best alternative. Boulder Bowl, located in the historic area of Boulder City at 504 California Avenue, has been operating since 1947 and is still family-owned, even with several changes in ownership. Diana and Lonnie Cavins were in charge, having purchased the business from Steve and Chris Osborne in 2012. It has been recently sold. It's small and retro (with eight

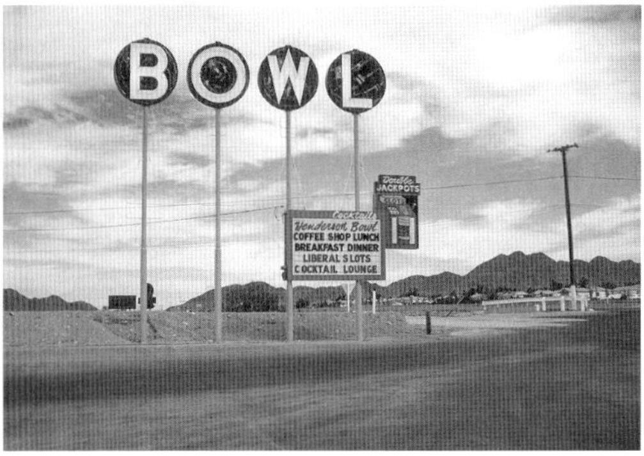

The vintage Henderson Bowl sign is long gone, but the memories remain. *Author's collection.*

wood lanes with above-lane ball returns, as many have experienced), and the folks operating the fully stocked snack bar are as attentive as ever. To its credit, this was also the only bowling alley in the area that supported the "Kids Bowl Free" summer program. The word most often used when describing this place is *quaint*, followed by references to *The Big Lebowski*. Henderson Bowling Alley closed some time ago, well before Stations Casinos took over bowling operations in this area. Details are sketchy, but some older area residents still remember the fun they had as children or teens attempting to throw the balls down the lanes with their friends or family. It would be good to have more information about this place, but at least there is a picture, courtesy of Henderson Libraries.

More "vintage" locals also fondly recall the Townsite Bowling Alley, built in the early '40s, when BMI was constructing conveniences for its residents. This was where you could enjoy some exercise on the lanes while quaffing a brew or soda during the evenings or weekends while sharing a snack with friends. As is the norm, all best-remembered activities had one thing in common: they involved finding common ground while breaking bread together. Patsy Ackerman shared that "the bowling alley had eight [wooden] lanes. My mom bowled there in the 1940s. It also had a pool hall. I babysat for the lady that ran the dinner counter." Mary Arkell also reiterated that the bowling alley had a café, not a snack bar. "My mom worked there when we first moved to Henderson in 1948." Simple fare was offered—nothing fancy, just basic light snacks such as burgers or dogs and fries, lunch dishes and perhaps sandwiches, as others recall. These easy-to-prepare snacks and small meals were enough to give energy to those throwing the balls on the lanes and the spectators cheering them on.

The Sizzler Steakhouse was a well-known family-run operation, and many locals recall visiting the place. It was a real treat to dine there with

Back in the day, the Townsite Bowling Alley was a thriving hangout for all ages, whether for bowling or for the snack bar and café. *Courtesy of the Henderson Library Digital Collection (HLDC), used with permission.*

their families. Folks still rave about the Malibu chicken, the toast, the bleu cheese dressing and the friendly service provided by the "Sizzlerettes." Located at 110 North Boulder Highway, the establishment closed due to bankruptcy in the 1990s. As Debra Avery shared, "I worked at Sizzler in 1976 for the Novtonys. It was privately owned by them. They had the best chicken fried steak in town. They would buy the meat from Tops market on Lake Mead." They did have cute uniforms of the hot pants variety, as photos show, but everyone remembered the friendly atmosphere and delicious food most of all.

Heather Eilene Carducci Kelley shared a few memories of her family's pizza restaurant, TK's World Famous Pizza (and yes, it delivered, as she made special mention). This little restaurant was owned by "my daddy, Terrance Kelley." This was a time when business opportunities were unlimited, and Terrance thrived on running the place while making a living for his family, providing fresh homemade thin- and thick-crust specialty pizzas for the masses. She was young at the time but does have a photo to share in memory of bygone days. Unfortunately, it wasn't clear enough to use, but it definitely shows the small white building standing proudly on its corner, with the words "World Famous Pizza" and the fact that it delivered clearly displayed. She said that her recollections of the restaurant are vague but fond and that her daddy was very proud of his little establishment.

Chapter 4

Closed for Business

Defunct Diners, Drive-Thrus and Drive-Ins

In the annals of time, few places are more fondly recalled than favorite haunts from your childhood and teen years. Nothing drives that nostalgia home more than the defunct diners, drive-thrus and drive-ins that you remember visiting with your family, the gang from school or on that first (or third) date. Such is also the case for many Henderson residents. Some of the popular places may have been discussed in the preceding chapters since these were often family-run operations, but they also deserve further notice in this chapter because of their obvious place in people's memories.

Of all the spots that are most avidly remembered, none has been mentioned more often or with more adamant words of praise than a little place that was simply known as Hot Dog Heaven.

Hot Dog Heaven was a unique little roadside pit stop located at 87 East Lake Mead Parkway. The place attracted a loyal following by offering a variety of delicious selections featuring everyone's favorite: the ubiquitous hot dog. Hot Dog Heaven offered quite a wide selection of dogs, from Vienna beef hot dogs to Polish sausage, Italian beef sandwiches, Italian sausage and more. This was the place folks dropped in to visit at least a few times a week for lunch or a snack, to either sit at the outside tables or to take out their food, until the business's unanticipated closure in late 2016. That is when the new landlord sold the property to a bank, and the owner walked away from the business…for a time. Touted by many as "the best hot dog in town," people rave about the Chicago dog ("pure deliciousness"), chili dogs, the crispy fries and the reasonable costs. This place was a veritable institution at this location for about twenty years, but if we are lucky and the rumors are correct, we may find this little hole-in-the-wall at another spot in the area in the not-too-distant future.

Rivaling Hot Dog Heaven are residents' memories of the Frostop drive-in, formerly at Lead and West Atlantic, across from Henderson Jr. High. Tia Martin had her own reason to recall the place with fondness: "My great-grandfather Owen Atkin used to own the Frostop in the '60s in Henderson. My parents used to work there when they were newlyweds. It was a hamburger place with carhops. My dad would work as a cook, and my mom was a carhop. When my mom describes the Frostop, it sounds like your typical late '50s and '60s hangout." The high school crowd from Basic school must have had a tough time choosing between this establishment with its burgers and milkshakes or Pac-Out's cheesy fries and tacos (not to mention the Dr Pepper!).

Dante's Drive-In, which stood in the same lot as Texaco and Basic Auto Parts (as many folks recall), holds a unique place in Henderson history. Not only did it feature some pretty good grub, but you could also get your car

Frostop Building and its iconic sign were a draw for the teen crowd back in the day, 1962. *City of Henderson Secure Files (copy of original), used with permission, photo #00882.*

parts at the next door Basic Auto Parts or have your vehicle serviced at the Texaco station in the lot while enjoying some delicious burgers at Dante's. There was some confusion about whether it was owned or operated by the same family, but it appears each business was separately run in the same general lot—the cooperation of businesses in the same general area just somehow worked. When the drive-in closed, Dante's continued on to be a beloved staple on Water Street. Its float joined others in city parades every year. Rick Watson (board member for the Henderson Historical Society) was quoted in an interview for Nevada Public Radio sharing:

> *Henderson was a really small town. Everybody knew everybody. There were no sidewalks in a lot of the town until I was almost out of high school. We would walk down to the old Victory Theater in the old Water Street District and rather than follow the streets we would just cut through everybody's yards. Maybe that's when they started building fences.... The Heritage Days celebration goes back to 1952. In 1952, it had been 10 years since the building of the BMI complex and since the building of the old town site. The city of Henderson decided to have a celebration to celebrate their tenth anniversary. It was such a success that they began to talk about making it an annual event* [retitling it the "Heritage Days" celebration rather than the Industrial Days, as in the past]. *The next year in 1953 they re-enacted the whole thing. They've done that every year since then.*

Dante's had a float in the first parade and in each one until the establishment closed—after all, according to their advertising and public opinion, they had "the best burgers in Southern Nevada." Sue had a different reason for remembering Dante's: "My mom, Carolyn Evans, along with Sally Vanhorn and Otta Rae Morrison, opened Dante's with owner Dan. Dante's later became Nicks Supper Club." James Cameron mused that "Dante's Drive-In was a little hamburger joint on Frontier Road, later Lake Mead Drive, just north of Water Street. It later became the Quickie Quickie Bar. Next door, Dante's Supper Club was built. I believe Joe Williams was the owner. This is what became Nick's Supper Club and was *very* successful." There may be a few conflicting memories from different individuals, which is normal with the passage of time and makes it more interesting, but the end result was that this place holds a fond spot in many different hearts.

Reminiscences by various residents includes the Whataburger that used to stand where the AM/PM is now located, on Boulder Highway

Dante's was a staple in the first Heritage Day parade and continued to make appearances for many years. *City of Henderson Secure Files (copy of original), used with permission.*

Dante's Drive-In and Texaco & Basic Auto Parts shared the parking lot. *City of Henderson Secure Files (copy of original), used with permission, photo #00374.*

and Lowery. Several locals remembered this one and Arctic Circle on the corner of Water Street and Victory Road, with Dinah Wells Epp touting both spots "as a great school lunch hang-out: with hamburgers as the draw." James Cameron also recalled the Polar Queen "on Water Street across from the Eldorado." All are fondly recalled as favorite gathering places for kids who were in their teens "back in the day." Friendly competition, indeed, for the hungry lunch crowd.

Times change. It has been said that for every action, there is an equal and opposite reaction. This is especially true of food establishments. Some places thrived, while others were simply a "flash in the pan." It could be due to a fleeting theme, fad, novel idea or just being in the wrong place at the wrong time. Whatever the reason, there were some other places that were neighborhood staples and had loyal clients before they closed. The following more recently closed establishments are definitely missed.

El Mero Mero Mexican Restaurant was nestled in the Boulder Marketplace strip mall at the corner of Boulder Highway and Major Avenue. It stood not far from where the 99c Store opened some while back, near where the ABC Food Store used to operate. This was a previously unmentioned establishment that only revealed itself in the form of a beautiful mural on the outside wall and a "Mexican Restaurant" sign with logo high above the door found when I went exploring early one Saturday morning. According to public records, it was privately owned, and by all reports, the prices were very reasonable for tasty dishes such as churros, beans and rice, enchiladas, tacos and other "West Coast" fare, as one source put it. It opened in 2007 and shut down a few

Jalisco Cantina store front and sign, as recalled by so many regulars. *Courtesy of a friend, author's collection.*

years later, in approximately 2010. No reason was given why, but it may have been economics because a number of other businesses in the same lot closed around the same time.

Noble Roman's Take-n-Bake Pizza, at 4140 East Sunset Road, had a great novel concept: design your own pizza on the premises (they even had a gluten-free crust!) and take it with you to bake at home. How convenient! It filled a previous niche that was lacking in a town of fast food, frozen meals at the supermarkets and a variety of regular pizza restaurants. Noble Roman's pizza was excellent, with delicious crusts and fresh, tasty toppings, but consistent traffic just wasn't there in this off-the-beaten-path location—probably because of the proximity of all the aforementioned fast-food joints and take-out pizza places, plus, as the company admitted, the length of lines due to the time taken to custom-design and prepare the pies. It hung on for a number of years to better serve the community before quietly shutting its doors for the last time in 2015. This place is fondly remembered by faithful patrons who enjoyed the cleanliness, the personal touches, a friendly staff and the convenience of "homemade" without the fuss. The pizzas are still available in the frozen section of various grocery stores in some parts of the country.

The Jalisco Cantina, at 3460 East Sunset Road Ste. D, was extremely popular with its Tex-Mex flavor and flair. Formerly known as Super Mex, this was another East Sunset restaurant that closed in 2017 with the decline of the mall and change in demographics. No matter what it was called, the reviews were consistently solid—great food at a decent price with wonderful service and a comfortable cantina dining/bar atmosphere that satisfied the crowds. No word on why it finally closed, but it was certainly enjoyed by locals who knew and appreciated it. It is still missed.

Chapter 5

Historic Landmarks and Casino Cafés

In days of yore, prior to the 1940s, Henderson was just a gleam in someone's eye, populated by farmers, ranchers and those who came over from other states to work at Boulder Dam and, later, at the BMI plant. There were long stretches of bare desert with nothing on them but sand, brush, scrub and desert tortoises. The roads were sand or gravel, and naturally, these were a lot less traveled than they are today and were sometimes even washed out by frequent sudden flash floods. This sense of being in the wild, the middle of nowhere, continued on into the '50s and even as late as into the '70s, as other locals have shared. Las Vegas resident Alan moved here in 1976, and his memories include a lot of open land and empty lots between what was here. "You would see a lot of cowboys on horseback riding along Lake Mead Blvd."

Living in Henderson back in the day meant proximity to Las Vegas and all it had to offer, including the excitement and glitz of the casinos on the Strip. It was only a matter of time until Henderson followed suit in order to enable residents to spend their hard-earned cash a little closer to home. With Green Valley being one of the first established master-planned communities in 1973, it was no surprise that in March 2000, the announcement was made that a large, luxurious casino/resort would be built in the area. Green Valley Ranch (in what is now known as the District at GVR) opened its doors a year later to much fanfare. By this time, city population had increased to more than 170,000 residents. This helped bridge the large desert gap between Las Vegas and Henderson.

Contrary to public belief, however, casinos have been thriving since the days of Pittman and Basic. The Alibi Club Casino was located in Pittman, Nevada, at 1120 North Boulder Highway. The casino opened in 1950 and closed in 1956 to reopen in 1959 (renovated?) before closing for good in 1962. It had "good eats and good gaming" quipped one longtime local.

Casinos like the Roadhouse, at 2100 North Boulder Highway, were the popular places to visit after a busy day at work or during the weekend, when the place really rocked. This was a neighborhood institution well before the bigger places moved in. The Roadhouse was originally called Stucky's and then the Goose and Gander before settling into its long life as a thriving casino, as shared by various folks. The remnants, including the iconic sign, are still left standing on the property while we wait to see whether it will be allowed to reopen since an initial attempt in 2010. Unfortunately, owner Robert McMackin's attempts to have a non-restricted casino have so far been stymied because in order to reopen and operate once again, there would have to be a two-hundred-room hotel built to meet compliance with competing casinos. We have yet to see this happen, but one can always hope.

The unique Rainbow Club Casino, at 122 South Water Street, was a neighborhood grocery store before becoming a casino in 1967. It was then purchased from the previous owner and opened as the Rainbow Club in 1984. There was once an upstairs movie theater where you would find all your favorite snacks and could catch the current movies of the day, remembered local resident Joyce Nunes. Jimmy Smerek also fondly recalled that the "Rainbow Club is a longtime downtown Henderson staple. Our grandfathers used to take us there. My girlfriend, Kaileen, and I didn't know each other then. They still have $1.99 breakfast specials." This is a pretty good deal considering you can get two eggs, bacon or sausage, hash browns and toast or biscuits and gravy on weekdays, with the cost being $2.39 on weekends! There are now forty-eight high-definition screens scattered throughout the casino that show scenes from around the world, as well as Sunday and Monday football for enthusiasts. Backing on the same street as the Emerald Island Casino (opened in 2003 after renovating a casino that had been defunct for three years) and close to the Eldorado (opened in 1962), this venerable trio have held their positions downtown for a long time. When you take a walk to the front of the building, you will be amazed at the brilliant mural and bright marquee that makes the exterior of the Rainbow Club distinctive.

It seems as though the Eldorado Casino (not the El Dorado, as many would have you believe), at 140 South Water Street, has been here

The Rainbow Club marquee shines, day or night, but sorry folks—breakfast is no longer served. *Photo by S. Damon, author's collection.*

"forever." Nestled in the heart of downtown Henderson, its signature name has proudly risen high into the skyline since the casino was built in 1962. In 1965, the owners bought the next door Royal Club, remodeling and doubling the casino's size. This old-school casino is well known throughout Las Vegas as being a true historic landmark. It was rebuilt from the shell of the former Wheel Casino, originally constructed in 1961, only to close just a year later. The purchase was considered to be a calculated risk given the area. Dining spots inside include Tequila Falls, a favorite "watering hole" for many visiting guests with its variety of margarita flavors, while the '50s themed Mary's Diner offers delicious burgers, thick shakes, malts and other diner fare that transported you back to simpler times. Or, as stated by a friend, "It's simply delicious."

The Emerald Island Casino, at 120 Market Street, holds its own in the area. This casino was opened in 2003 on the site of an unspecified casino that had taken over once the old Lucky Star closed (having been in operation from 1957 to 1972). So, Lucky Star first, then another unnamed place and finally Emerald Island, as it's been explained to me. That is quite the legacy! The beautifully painted exterior with its vibrant colors and imaginative artwork invites you into what can only be described as a patron-favorite penny casino that serves some of the tastiest, heartiest food in the area at its Emerald Island Grille. The Irish flavor is due to the owner Tim Brook's mother's roots. Frequent guest Donna Sunshine Caldwell described it as a friendly place where folks get to know one another and where you are always welcome. No wonder it's been a consistent "Best of Las Vegas" favorite. The servers are really attentive, and this is true "stick to your ribs" fare. There are lighter dishes—half a cantaloupe with delicious chicken salad in it, for example—but most guests love the all-day breakfasts. Its little breakfast skillet is outstanding with toast or with biscuits and gravy, and its burgers are

The Eldorado, the first of the trifecta of venerable casinos in the Market/Water area of downtown Henderson, still holding its head high since its opening in 1962. *Photo by S. Damon, author's collection.*

well worth the visit. Recommendations have flooded in for the "Breakfast Feast," "French Dip," "Whole Hog" (pulled pork, ham, bacon, BBQ sauce and dill pickle chips on a toasted bun) and the delicious signature baby back ribs. If you really want a neighborhood bar atmosphere "where everyone knows your name," this is the place to frequent. The best description would probably be "comfortable."

Mystic Falls was a friendly little casino at 920 South Boulder Highway. The small Mystic Falls Café offered a variety of tasty food with decent prices and was always humming. We enjoyed visiting the place and found it to be inviting and comfortable and were surprised to see it had closed around 2010. But to be honest, with all the competition, business did seem to be declining. The hostess said it had been quietly going under for a while. It was sold and survived briefly as My Lodge Casino then My Casino (slight changes on the sign) before succumbing and closing for good. It eventually morphed into the more popular Boulder Lodge before its newest incarnation as the (My) Points! and then Points casino, which no longer appears to be in operation. The location coupled with licensing restrictions and competition from so many larger established casinos in the area seems to have made it all but impossible for a small establishment to survive in this part of Henderson.

In the meantime, the venerable Skyline Casino and its café at 1741 North Boulder Highway continues, with many past and ongoing renovations to make it more attractive and appealing to tourists and locals in the fight to be competitive with nearby spots. It had history as the Dixie Bar prior to its purchase in 1964 by the current owner's father, who helped built the new Skyline. Research showed that the Dixie Bar was in operation from the 1940s (when the area was still known as Pittman) until 1964. Barton W. and Dorothy Dukett were the first owners. Rolly and Ella Cook purchased the bar in 1952, when it featured sandwiches as the main attraction. Ella also

One of the best features of the parking lot entrance at the Skyline Hotel and Casino is the neon cowboy waving "Howdy" to guests. This is one of the true features of "Old Vegas" at its finest. *Photo by S. Damon, author's collection.*

set up Cook's Books, a type of lending library for their vast stock of books, making this the only library in a local tavern. By 1957, there were four hundred books available, and customers suggested charging a small fee, with proceeds going to charity. This was established, and the profits purchased playground equipment for local children.

The couple retired in 1960, and the bar was purchased by John Lagouri and his business partners, including Frank Kish and Joseph Antonio. They built the four-thousand-square-foot Skyline Casino & Restaurant on the premises. The grand opening was a gala three-day event, beginning at 6:00 a.m. on October 1, 1964. The twenty-four-hour restaurant served Chinese, Italian and American food, with a seating capacity of ninety-six people. It closed in 1965 for "remodeling" and was purchased by Walter Stogsdill in 1968, closing a few months later. Lagouri reopened the place in 1974. It had once again been completely remodeled, and there were unrealized plans for a sports book and a forty-unit motel. John Kish took over the reins in 1975. Jim Marsh purchased it in 2003 and has been working on it ever since then. By 1996, the building had been expanded to thirty thousand square feet. With all the changes in ownership, the ongoing state of flux and renovations—even to this day, with a new hotel tower (which has been described as "amazing")—this casino is finally realizing its potential and regaining its popularity as compared with Emerald Isle and Eldorado.

The fondest memories, however, held by longtime residents are of the place "doing some serious business back in the day" with its unique appearance and great location. It is a relief that the original exterior façade has been maintained throughout. When you drive around the building to the parking lot in the back, this is a true throwback to casinos of the '50s or '60s with the single-story design, striped awnings and the neon cowboy waving at you to enter. It stands in complete contrast to its modern hotel tower next door. The busy "retro red booths" in the restaurant also prove that the Skyline is still apparently going strong, offering a diner-like atmosphere with good stick-to-your-ribs food, including prime rib, its "under $2.00" breakfast specials and tasty, healthier soups and salads.

Mugshots was "where the Leaning Tower of Pizza used to be," as Jimmy Smerek and Joyce Nunes recalled. According to sources, the Leaning Tower of Pizza was a hangout for headliners owned and operated by mob member Jasper Speciale. Mugshots, to the contrary, was a favorite watering hole for residents. A few other contacts remembered Mugshots Eatery/Bar Sportsbook as having stood at 1120 North Boulder Highway. One person remembered it as being a "dive," while another recalled it as "having a cool atmosphere" and decent prices for reasonably tasty food. Whatever the name during its run and however jumbled the recollections, the establishment is worth including for the memories.

Folks also remember the Dust Jug, a suitably named bar that served liquid libation to thirsty desert-dwellers as well as tasty bar food. Those who recalled the place asked that it also be included even though very little—including the actual location—is remembered. The consensus was that it was on Boulder Highway. In the days when the road was gravel and the weather hot, this place attracted locals and lived up to its name—a place to wet your whistle for a little while.

The Ranch House Bar used to stand at Boulder Highway and Lake Mead (the site of Roberto's). This place was recommended as notable by a few locals, but there were no details forthcoming about menus or atmosphere. From all accounts, it was a comfortable albeit noisy place to gather for a few drinks in the evenings or on the weekends with your buddies.

The only known photo of the Branding Bar Casino was in the paper, after a plane crash on April 10, 1965. One person mentioned the place as having a good café and comfortable atmosphere, and suggesting it to a few groups did jog some vague memories. It was another old-timer from "back in the day."

The Henderson Public Library has a photo of the Bliss Restaurant after a flood on July 24, 1955. No one seems to recall the business, but the proof is in the photo. Las Vegas and Henderson were notorious for flash floods before modern washes were created to help out with the runoff. In fact, we sometimes still get them after a torrential rainfall during monsoon season. As one fascinating flood report stated:

> *The Las Vegas area was swamped for the second time on the same day by a violent cloudburst on Sunday, July 24. Floodwater swept down on Henderson, swamping hundreds of homes and shutting off traffic on the Boulder Highway. Hours after the cloudburst, a flood struck Las Vegas with tremendous fury, causing moderate damage to areas of the City already hard hit by the flash flood June 13. Most of the afternoon deluge centered on Tract Number Two on the east end of Henderson, where residents tried to slow down the rising tide by throwing up wooden barricades. Water as high as four feet deep flooded homes, leaving deposits of silt throughout the tract. Also hit hard by the flood were Victory Village and Carver Park. The Henderson Street Department worked far into the night to repair damaged streets and to remove mud from easements in the three inundated housing developments. Water sweeping down from Tract Number Two closed the highway south of Henderson and other floodwaters cut off the Pittman Highway approach. U.S. Highway 93-95-466 was closed to traffic for nearly two hours, and highway patrolmen were stopping cars as far away as Railroad Pass. Jean and Mountain Pass were also hit by rainstorms, but U.S. Highway 91 was still open.*

This was truly a major event in Henderson history, especially with two drenchings within the same day, and it's good that they did flood reports in order to preserve the memories.

PLACES OF INTEREST: LANDMARKS

Ron Lee's World of Clowns Factory Tour, at 330 Carousel Parkway off Warm Springs Road, was a popular attraction opened by the talented artist—the creator of the famous "Hobo Joe"—to offer locals the opportunity to enjoy the learning process and the chance to purchase his trademark original soft-metal hand-painted clowns. He absolutely loved the circus and used his well-honed talents for the "lost wax" process and for animation. The entrance to the factory had his own "Ronnie World," a miniature amusement park fully appointed with tiny lit rides and little people to welcome you into his establishment. It took a while to track this down and put it all together, but it appears to be the same business that Joyce Nunes remembered. "There was an artist who did, I believe, Disney art for the California movie studios. He had a shop/display/studio on Warm Springs/Marks where he sold figurines and so on. The public could go in and browse for free, buy art or eat. It was called the Carousel, and there was a restaurant, the Carousel Restaurant."

This place only exists in the memories of a few longtime residents like Joyce, and details have been lost with the years. But it sounded like an establishment that could definitely have been popular in its day. The "Clown Factory" holds a fascinating mystery—a story that begs inclusion in any book on Henderson. Lee had a magnificent factory custom-built at this location. The building featured a plate glass wall with a hallway allowing the public to enjoy free half-hour self-guided factory tours (with or without a clown escort). The tour took you from the design and casting through the finishing processes. The World of Clowns was well set back off the beaten path between bald patches of unused land, demonstrating Lee's preference for isolation. It has been speculated that the whole parcel of land bordered by West Warm Springs Road, North Gibson Road, Kelso Dunes Avenue and Marks Street was owned by Ron Lee. The only building on this huge parcel was his factory.

He was purported to be a bit of a recluse who liked the isolation while keeping his inner child alive, so no one really understands why he even would have moved his family here and constructed a spectacular new building when he subsequently shut down operation not fifteen years later to go back to California. Mind you, by that time he was working on animation projects for Disney, so maybe the move home made sense to him and his loved ones. Other than the popular tour, the facility also had display cases for his clown statues, clown memorabilia on the walls, a large gift shop, a cafeteria featuring a "luncheon style menu," administrative offices and a beautiful thirty-foot-wide jewel-encrusted "Chance" carousel that was roped off and didn't appear to ever be in operation, even though rides were offered for one dollar. For a quarter, guests could enjoy his collection of carnival rides near the back of the gallery, where green dragons carried tiny people around and around or flying elephants with pink cheeks soared through the air while a gold-plated Ferris wheel shone with a "myriad of colors," according to a newspaper article. The business operated from 1994 to 2008. After that time, by all accounts the whole operation was suddenly packed up and moved back to the original Burbank, California site, where Lee continued working on his projects. Nothing else has been recorded about the Henderson factory or grounds. Ron Lee passed away on February 26, 2017, so the mystery may never be solved.

Kidd & Company Marshmallow Factory (aka the Kraft Marshmallow Factory), at 1180 Marshmallow Lane, gave eager guests of all ages a glimpse into the production of everyone's favorite puffy treat. The Kidd family offered self-guided tours down a long hallway with a huge glass window you could peer through, letting you look into the factory area to see how marshmallows were made. At the end of the tour, guests were given a four-ounce bag of the latest marshmallows and could buy merchandise and treats in the factory gift store. The factory was rebuilt after the 1988 PEPCON explosion and fire, after which area residents still recall the "campfire smell" of burning marshmallows in the air. Everyone mused how a chemical plant and marshmallow manufacturer coexisted next door to each other. Once the factory was rebuilt, the marshmallows kept rolling off the Kidd Company conveyor belts until 1996, when the operation was sold to Favorite Brands. A more efficient production line was installed, making the old production line obsolete and therefore seldom put in use. Disappointed guests could no longer watch marshmallows being made.

In 1999, Nabisco Foods purchased Favorite Brands, and the factory tours were permanently closed. Before that time, an average of about 500,000 guests per year had watched the factory in operation. When Philip Morris Companies Inc.—the parent company of Kraft Foods—bought out Nabisco Foods, it took over the marshmallow manufacturing. In 2001, operations ceased and the equipment was dismantled and shipped to other locations as the factory was closed, with the building being put up for sale. To this day, tourists still ask where the factory is and if they can take the tour. Apparently, the Clown Museum, Kidd's Marshmallow Factory and Ethel M Chocolates were the trifecta of Henderson tours for locals and visitors.

Chapter 6

Gone but Not Forgotten

Unique Local Favorites

Food remains a constant in our memories. The scents, the textures and the flavors trigger so many fond recollections. We remember home-cooked meals, family dinners, recipes and the special places we used to go out to dine with parents and friends. We also remember places we visited on special occasions: celebrations, birthdays, Christmas Eve, Thanksgiving, Mother's or Father's Day and more. And then there are places that highlight special times in our childhood and benchmark our growth into adulthood. Local Henderson residents are no exception. They are adamant about their favorites: the Frostop, Hot Dog Heaven, Pac-Out, Arctic Circle, Whataburger, Nick's Supper Club, the Gold Mine and more.

Apparently, there also used to also be a very popular Crystal Palace Skating Rink on Lake Mead that served food as well as gave kids the chance to skate their day or evening away, according to another local. But there can only be one clear-cut winner that was truly a unique gathering place for families and friends, especially during the holiday season. There has never been and never will be a spot with the exact same ambiance and flair, the same outstanding décor and unique environment. This chapter is dedicated to the memory of Hershel Leverton's creation, Alpine Village Inn. Rediscover this blast from the past (you may even be tempted to re-create the soup) as you read shared memories with the addition of a recipe from its heyday.

A good friend, Krista Demenezes, was the first person to tell me about this place. She and her family used to frequent it for family dinners when she was young. She fondly remembered it as housing three stories: the basement with its sawdust floors (complete with peanuts!) and plank tables for "family-style dining"; the main floor with cuckoo clocks "all over the place"; and the second floor with its massive train sets (for the child in all of us). It was featured in a newspaper article by the *Review-Journal* as one of the most memorable places in town. While not technically *in* Henderson, it was definitely so near and dear to so many locals that it begs inclusion as the exception to the rule as a favorite spot set "just outside the city line" in Paradise, Nevada.

ALPINE VILLAGE INN

Once upon a time, there was a unique destination that was truly a Las Vegas institution: Alpine Village Inn. It began its long life downtown in 1950, moving four times before settling into its home on Paradise Road, just across from the Las Vegas Hilton (now the Westgate) in 1970. The main floor could seat 250 diners and looked like a Bavarian village, with attentive waiters in lederhosen and waitresses in long skirts.

The basement held the Rathskeller, a bar and sandwich shop with the requisite peanuts on the floor. You could sing along to traditional German drinking songs played by the piano player (one friend fondly recalled the children's favorite "Schnitzelbank" song with comic twists: "*Ist dast nicht eine schnitzelbank? Yah, dast ich eine schnitzelbank!*"; it was popular back in the day). Guests—from families to the enthusiastic undergrads from UNLV—loved the novelty and nostalgia created by this part of the restaurant.

The whole place, from roof to basement, was built like an alpine chalet with a sloped roof, bright welcoming colors, Swiss clocks, big-game trophies, Alpen horns, cow bells and the memorable, impressive train set. Folks from all over the valley would journey to the restaurant to enjoy its *gemütlichkeit* (fellowship, warmth, welcome or good cheer). This restaurant ruled the Las Vegas area until closing in March 1997, and it has not been forgotten, even after more than twenty years since its demise. Friends have said that their childhood Christmas Eve never was the same after its closure. As is the case with any memorable dining place, folks remember their favorite dishes, which leads to much lively discussion and debate. At Alpine Village, it was the food: the famous chicken soup and unique seasoned cottage cheese (so in demand that it was also bagged for sale in the gift shop), not to mention the huge baked potatoes just begging to be devoured—the food was the highlight of every visit. The soup was served steaming hot in heavy pewter bowls, and the cottage cheese was accompanied by mini loaves of pumpernickel and/or rye bread. The *Las Vegas Review Journal* published some of the recipes after the restaurant closed, so now you can enjoy a taste of the Alpine Village Inn anytime you like.

Chicken Supreme Soup (serves 6 to 8)

From the Alpine Village Inn
(courtesy of the *Las Vegas Review Journal*)

Soup:

2 quarts water
2 teaspoons celery salt
2 teaspoons Accent
1 pound ground chicken, cooked
1 medium onion, ground
yellow food coloring (optional)
2 teaspoons salt
¼ teaspoon pepper
1 teaspoon Kitchen Bouquet
2 tablespoons chicken bouillon
2 carrots, ground up

Roux:

½ cup vegetable oil
1 cup all-purpose flour

Preparation

To prepare, boil all soup ingredients together for about 30 minutes. Remove pot from heat and let cool slightly. Ladle mixture into a blender, 2 to 3 cups at a time, and blend until almost smooth. Pour back into large pot. To prepare the roux, heat the vegetable oil until just smoking. Remove from heat, add the flour and stir with a wire whisk. The oil and flour roux should be the consistency of mashed potatoes. Add the roux to the soup and simmer until thick, using a wire whisk to blend so it doesn't scorch. This gives the soup the creamier texture. Serve hot and enjoy. (To reheat, use low heat and stir constantly to avoid lumps.)

Chapter 7

The Survivors

Despite all the changes in population dynamics—with current numbers exceeding 250,000 residents—the boom in growth of the area of the city of Henderson to approximately 108 miles as of 2017 and the new businesses constantly opening and catching the eye of patrons, some places have managed to not just survive but thrive. Faced with competition from other sources, including the ever-present casinos, a few spots have had to change with the times—changing décor, changing venues, trying different approaches and options—while others simply hold true to their roots and withstand the test of time. And then again, there were those that weren't quite so successful despite giving it their best shot. Various areas of town seem to be affected more with the shift in patrons' tastes and expectations and, to be honest, with rising costs and property values. Here's to the survivors and also a nod to those establishments that gave it their all and still didn't quite make it.

One of the most popular survivors in the older part of Henderson is Johnny Mac's, located, as always, at 842 South Boulder Highway. This is a neighborhood bar that is still very much alive and kickin'. Standing in the strip mall at the busy corner of North Boulder Highway and Major Avenue, Johnny Mac's deserves recognition as an enduring small casino and bar offering treats such as buffalo wings, New York–style pizza (half price on Wednesdays), the self-touted "best in town" corned beef and cabbage (the Tuesday special) plus other nightly specials including homemade meatloaf on Monday, two-for-one pasta on Thursday and the ever-popular Haddock

Fish Fry on Friday, all prepared by Chef Thiery Balin. There's a long bar inside with inset gaming machines to try your luck, plus booths and tables to suit your fancy. Framed sports jerseys, memorabilia and photos adorn the wooden walls, and it just has that friendly air about it. John McGinty has been successfully running the place in the same location for more than three decades now (which says a lot for customer loyalty and a great venue, as well as true grit). It still hums when the canvas walls roll up and the crowd—younger and older—spills onto the sidewalk tables to take advantage of balmy spring and summer evenings. Then the whole area seems to come alive with laughter and music.

Friendly Donut House, at 856 South Boulder Highway, is an unprepossessing little donut shop nestled in the Henderson Shopping Center—the Smith's strip mall. This place has won several "Best of Las Vegas" awards, and the donuts are legendary. If you drop in during the evening, you may have to wait for the sweet little man to appear from the back, where he is busy crafting those fluffy delights, but it's well worth the short delay as you stand marveling at the glazed, chocolate, powdered, sprinkled delights or the crullers, huge apple fritters, custard-filled maple bars (only on weekends, by all reports), donut holes (highly recommended!) and other treats. It's not a fancy shop and there is not really much in the way of seating, but the cost is very decent for these simple but delectable treats. Mr. and Mrs. Lim work day and night eleven months of the year to prepare everyone's favorites, and we appreciate it! Everyone who loves donuts seems to agree that you don't know tasty until you try Friendly's. Locals in Vegas and Henderson recognize this place and the pink box very well. It's not uncommon for favorite selections to be sold out by closing, despite the little man's diligence in working hard every evening to keep cases stocked. Don't forget your wallet, as it is cash only.

Coo Coo's Gourmet Coffee Café, at 7482, 19 Pacific Avenue, is an example of an establishment that has chosen to change with the times in order to survive. Evolving from a simple coffee shop featuring homemade goodies and simple brewed coffee, this small place now offers java drinks, light lunch fare (salads, soups and sandwiches) and free Wi-Fi for those who want a quiet place to catch up with what's going on in their world or even for students who want to find a nook in which to study. New management "changed things up" by making this a comfortable spot for friends to meet and relax while enjoying a signature brew or something tasty to sink your teeth into. There are daily specials, so check the board and don't forget to ask. Coo Coo's has definitely found its niche. It's tiny, it's cute and it's in a great location, nestled into the row of small shops on Pacific.

The Gold Mine Tavern, at 23 South Water Street, has risen like a phoenix from the ashes several times during the years it has been in business. For a long time, this was simply just a little neighborhood bar as it was during the twenty-seven years Ron Oliverra owned the place. His wife, Toni, recalled him talking about the *Cheers*-like atmosphere and the awesome Motherlode sandwiches in the Grubsteak Sandwich Shop. There was a decline for a number of years after Ron and Toni left, when it became a hangout for motorcycle gangs and gained a rough reputation with bad reviews, but new ownership has been working to revive the place with open mic night, live bands on the patio featuring a variety of genres of music offered nightly, no cover and specials. The Gold Mine is proving that you can have a modern-day coffee house/bar with a twist. Mind you, with all the renovations touted in the vicinity on Water Street, it's also about location, location, location!

Chef Flemming's Bake Shop, at 7 South Water Street Ste. B, is a small European-style bakery in the historic Water Street District of Henderson. This little shop with big flavor has been at its location for about ten years now, according to the lovely woman who assisted us. The delicious pastries—cookies, eclairs, macarons, cupcakes, mini cheesecakes, crumb cakes and so on—are fresh and beautifully presented. But, ah, the bread. Friday is rye bread day, and even though we couldn't get the marble rye due to our late arrival, the rye bread without seeds (our choice) and the pumpernickel were delectable. This was our second visit in two days because we loved the egg twists and eclairs so much the previous time. Chef Flemming Pederson is not just a certified executive pastry chef with a wealth of experience and training. He served his apprenticeship and graduated from the Danish Laug and then worked at various bakeries across the United States, after immigrating here, before becoming executive pastry chef at the four-star Golden Nugget. Chef Flemming shared his love for his craft on his PBS program *Chef's Class*, donates his considerable talent to the "Blue Star Mothers" of Henderson and Boulder City in support of our troops and passes on his love for his craft as an instructor at the International Culinary School at the Art Institute of Las Vegas. From all accounts, his wedding and birthday cakes are also little works of art in their own right and well known throughout the Valley. The shop opens at 7:00 a.m. on Tuesdays through Fridays and closes at 5:00 p.m. during the week and operates from 7:00 a.m. to 4:00 p.m. on Saturday. In a word, "yum."

Sunset Pizzeria, at 203 South Water Street, is unique: an excellent pizza establishment nestled within a bar hidden in plain sight in a downtown historic building. There are three locations of Sunset Pizzeria in Henderson, but this is the one that piqued our interest. The chefs make the dough from

The Historic Pinnacle Building houses the Sunset Pizzeria. There are also two other Sunset locations on Boulder Highway and East Sunset in Henderson, but this one has to have the most atmosphere.

scratch daily on premises from the finest ingredients, and it's evident in the taste. The pizza sauce is blended from the finest Italian herbs and spices; they use 100 percent Mozzarella cheese, imported 100 percent olive oil and fine herbs; and the toppings are primo to create the perfect pizza. They even make their own ranch dip for salads or dipping your crusts! Other menu items include strombolis and calzones, chicken wings and fingers, gyros, burgers, Philly steaks and grinders, subs and sandwiches, pastas, salads, appetizers and dessert. Pretty impressive for a bar setting. The other two locations are in storefront restaurants, but Mike Zakis, the owner, was pleased to have a downtown Henderson location, set in the historic Pinnacle Building after the short-lived Berwick's closed at the end of 2013. Zakis opened this new location in the spring of 2014, and it's been hopping ever since with bar, karaoke, gaming and, yes, some of the best pizza in town.

Kyklos Greek Café has found its niche in the food court of the Galleria at Sunset since its establishment in 2002. This popular kiosk offers authentic Greek and Mediterranean dishes created by three brothers: Sophocles, Constantine and Yiannis Frangakis. They opened the restaurant to honor their parents, Christos and Anastasia, as a tribute to the fine Greek food on which they were raised and remembered so fondly. Their parents are not around to help with the restaurant, but their legacy exists in the food selections and the menu. All the brothers have had extensive training at various establishments on the Strip. Sophocles ("Soph") now runs the café, still serving the popular gyro, souvlaki, pitas, lamb, spanakopita, dolmathes and other delicious fare, often accompanied by the outstanding tzatziki sauce. And don't forget the hummus and Kalamata olives! This kiosk is always a gathering place for those who love real quality Greek food at affordable prices. The mall location makes it accessible to all ages and stages, and the aroma of the food entices you to walk that way. When folks are looking for a meeting place, Kyklos is the obvious choice.

According to sources, the Rose Garden Chinese Restaurant, at 14 West Pacific Avenue, was once called the San Pan in its previous life. Since it changed management in 2011, sole owner and operator, Mei Kai, has shared the flavors and dishes she remembered from her home country with fans in the Water Street District. Her previous Chinese restaurant was in Chinatown on Spring Mountain Road, but according to sources, she made the move to this location in order to have the luxury of time to personalize her service and get to know her patrons. Many locals consider this to be one

Rose Garden Chinese Restaurant meals are touted as being the "most authentic Chinese food" to be found in Henderson. The Rose Garden is nestled in a strip of shops on Water Street in the historic area of downtown Henderson, but don't be fooled by the appearance—the inside is beautifully decorated and inviting and the welcome is warm. *Photo by S. Damon, author's collection.*

of the most authentic Chinese restaurants in town. This small, nondescript (on the outside) casual dining establishment, nestled in a strip of businesses in downtown Henderson—next to a chiropractor's office—gives you the option to enjoy meals on premises, get your food delivered or enjoy takeout. The menu offers delicious combination plates to allow you the chance to try a variety of dishes, or you may prefer the lunch or family dinner options. Prices are reasonable, and you can select from hot pot items, bowls, plates, appetizers, entrées, soups, vegetable dishes, many chicken-based options, beef or seafood. The chef's specials—such as Kung Pao triple, Happy Family and the Meat or Seafood Wor Bar—are enough to guarantee repeat visits. This is Chinese food done right with an authentic taste and delicious ingredients in a comfortable casual dining atmosphere that is "old school" in the best possible way, according to those in the know.

The El Torito, at 2126 South Boulder Highway, may not look very impressive from the outside, but it's a true survivor with real Mexican flair

The El Torito building exterior may look plain, but the flavor is still happening inside, where the granddaughter of the original owner keeps the business thriving. Owner Betty Pilon and her husband had a dream when she opened El Torito all those years ago. Her photo is still displayed by the register. *Photo by S. Damon, author's collection.*

This colorful mural has graced the walls of the El Torito for years, welcoming patrons as they celebrate its sixty-plus years of Henderson heritage. *Photo by S. Damon, author's collection.*

and has recently been remodeled inside. According to patrons who frequent the place, the Tex-Mex food is always tasty and the flavor authentic. Perhaps that is why this family-run establishment has passed ownership down from generation to generation, surviving since 1975. Bette Pilon was the original owner, pursuing her dream to open her own establishment in Henderson. After her death in 1988, her legacy was passed on to her daughter, Denise Pilon Colletti. Bette's granddaughter Gina Pilon Colletti proudly took over the reins fifteen years ago and is still running the place. She pointed out that the original owners' photo is still prominently displayed on the wall beside the register, and the beautiful mural adds distinct ambiance to the small dining area. The taco shells have always been homemade, and portions of all entrées are large with a decent price. Friends rave about the chips, salsa, soup and enchiladas. It's satisfying to see a small establishment be so well known in the community and to have it succeed for so long while drawing a loyal set of clients. This is the true flavor of Henderson.

The Omelet House, at 316 North Boulder Highway at Lake Mead, was opened by Fred Ostertag in 1992. He was one of the owners of the original establishment in Las Vegas. Since the day the doors opened, the vintage decorations and displayed "treasures" all make you feel at home (which is why his wife, Kelly, chose them for the restaurant), but what brings you back is the delicious variety of food. With omelets as its specialty you would expect a huge number of choices, and there is indeed no lack of items on the menu. You can go from "baby" to double (huge) servings that allow you to choose the meats, cheeses, veggies, number of eggs used and other fillings of your preference. With names like the Kitchen Sink, Farmer Juan, the Loch-Ness Monster, the Toadstool, the Cowboy Special and the Bugsy Siegel, you can see that a sense of humor as well as a sense of what makes tasty real is what kept this place running for so long. Waffles, pancakes, stuffed French toast (yum!), eggs Benedict, breakfast specials and oatmeal are all hearty and mighty tasty. And then there are lunchtime offerings, including the Monster Burger and the Monster Omelette, which have made a name for themselves with returning patrons. If you can finish the three-pound Monster Burger alone, you get a T-shirt and your name on the wall for posterity's sake. Other lunch delights are the homemade soups and a large number of sandwiches (including the Philly and the new Hot Pastrami). Open from 7:00 a.m. to 3:00 p.m. every day except Thanksgiving and Christmas, you can keep going back and back without ever repeating a menu item—unless you want to, of course! We could have made a meal of the potato spuds alone but didn't, so bring your appetite.

Yes, Virginia, you can make chocolate in the desert and eat it too! In 1981, Forrest Mars Sr. (yes, of *that* Mars family) opened the Ethel M Chocolate Factory and store at 2 Cactus Garden Drive, the corner of Sunset Road and

Ethel M Chocolate Factory & Botanical Cactus Garden. *Author's collection.*

Mountain Vista. This was a sort of "retirement project" for the chocolate pioneer, and he named it in honor of his mother, Ethel. Mars wanted to start a chocolate factory in Nevada because this was one of the few places he could legally sell his liqueur chocolates, and besides, he loved the desert and cacti. He also intended to showcase his mother's chocolate recipes, originally made in the kitchen of their home when he was still a young child. Mr. Mars lived in a penthouse suite above the factory for some years in order to check on the chocolate making progress and to interact with guests from around the city, the country and, eventually, around the world.

Different approaches were tried throughout its years of operation: Ethel's Lounge with its lounge area, chocolate fondue and fruit; the opportunity to have your chocolate custom-designed; Ethel brand chocolates (a short run of delicious designer gourmet chocolates designed by Jin Caldwell, master chocolatier and an artist in her own right); and other endeavors. But the traditional treats as first made in his mother's kitchen from her recipes still used to this day have always been the most popular. His cactus garden grew and grew until it became the botanical wonder it is today, with its massive solar garden nestled in the midst.

The new flagship shop (at the same location) opened in November 2016 and is more than twice the size of the old shop. It includes a Tasting Room Experience at the front entrance (so much fun learning to appreciate the different flavors and textures in several different pieces), with a few new twists that have to be experienced to be believed, and a new chocolate fountain just inside the shop entrance that is a marvel to behold. (Tastings are also held at the High Roller on the Strip, but the entire experience is only available at the Factory Store.) Directly to the right of the Tasting Room door is the tour aisle, where you can see the machinery necessary for production, with those huge vats of melted milk, white and dark chocolate, and you may be able to catch a glimpse of production through the glass and perhaps even see the ever-popular Mars Bar or pecan brittle in the works. As one guest quipped, "It's clean enough to eat off the floor!" In answer to a popular question, yes, they really do make chocolate in the factory. The tour aisle has been designed to be wheelchair accessible, with the new design raising the ramp to permit easier viewing for young guests as well. This leads you to the upper demo area, where, to everyone's delight, you can watch chocolatiers dipping strawberries, marshmallows and pretzels, which you can then choose from to purchase. At the bottom of the ramp and stairs, turn right to reach the main shop area, with two counters where you can design your own specialty box of chocolates or purchase prepacked selections.

There is also a small beverage counter where you can purchase snacks or beverages, including the "real" hot chocolate. It's legendary—melted chocolate and steamed milk with whipped cream. The milkshake is a recent addition to the menu and has to be experienced to be believed (think chocolate brittle and ice cream!). Ethel M's preservative-free chocolate has a loyal client base, both in person and online, while thousands of tourists flock to the site every day by car and tour bus. At Christmastime, the cactus garden is festooned with more than 1 million lights adorning the cacti, trees and bushes. It is free and a sight to behold, as it has become a tradition for many families to stroll the garden, see the lights and decorations, sip hot chocolate and, now, "ice skate" during the holiday season on a plexiglass rink. The garden is still a sanctuary to a wide variety of critters—including birds, tiny lizards and other wild residents—so no pets are allowed. Service animals on a leash may be permitted outside.

Chapter 8

The Boulder City Connection and Lake Las Vegas

Boulder City has been like a home away from home since Henderson was a struggling industrial town, drawing visiting workers from all over the country to help it grow into a thriving city. The reverse has also always run true, with Boulder City residents enjoying all that Henderson has to offer, especially since casinos are not permitted within the Boulder City limits. The connection between the cities is evident when you look up many businesses between Henderson and Boulder City: they come up listed as in "Henderson" in the phone directories. Boulder City is just a ten- to fifteen-minute scenic drive from downtown Henderson via Lake Mead Boulevard or a more direct route using Boulder Highway, but it is a totally different world once you travel the eleven miles or so to get there. This is most definitely small-town Nevada all the way, with an estimated population of under sixteen thousand residents. It's somewhat difficult to envision driving through barren desert and gravel roads cut through sheer mountains along Boulder Highway all those years ago, with nothing much around or ahead of you, but there are reminders. The tall rock faces, the proximity of Hoover Dam, the mountain sheep that like to come down from the hills to graze and observe you as you picnic at Hemenway Park and the scenic beauty of Lake Mead (a lake on the Colorado River), plus the quaint historic district of Boulder City, all bring home what it must have been like during the construction of the Hoover Dam in the '30s. However, to get to the town itself, you first have to pass by a well-known legendary site unique to this region: Railroad Pass, steeped in history and with a brand-new highway all its own for better access!

RAILROAD PASS

Few places are nearer and dearer to area residents than the legendary Railroad Pass Casino. With decent menu prices for working folks and the chance to try your luck at the slots, it was a natural fit and a homey change from the more glitzy casinos on- and off-Strip. This is still the case, but traveling that seemingly endless road to and from back in the day must have been a far cry from the journey we now enjoy. When you see that sign high up on the mountain and turn the final corner to get a glimpse of the casino itself, it's well worth the short jog from town.

Railroad Pass, at 2800 South Boulder Highway, first opened on August 1, 1931, the same year gambling was legalized in Nevada. The first train journeying through the mountain heading toward the future Hoover Dam site also carried the lumber used to build this casino. It was the third casino licensed in this state and is touted as the longest continuously running licensed casino in the United States. By adapting and growing with the times, while remaining true to its history and roots, Railroad Pass has remained a staple favorite destination (even with the tale of the ghost train that parents still tell their children).

Residents from Henderson, Las Vegas, Searchlight and Boulder City all enjoy its proximity, especially since gambling was and is still prohibited in the Greater Boulder City area. Nestled firmly in the "safe zone," it is easy to see why this comfortable and homey casino is as popular as ever. The food is delicious in the Iron Rail Café no matter when you visit (open 24/7), and there are also late-night specials—sometimes as low as $1.99—great for truckers, campers or travelers headed to and from Lake Mead or other destinations. From personal experience, the burgers are huge and delicious, and the country-fried steak and eggs is scrumptious! Costs are very reasonable. The Three Deuces Breakfast comes highly recommended with its French toast, eggs and bacon or sausage for under $5.00. The Boxcar Buffet is everyone's favorite: salad and dessert bars, "Live Action Stations" on Friday/Saturday/Sunday and a very reasonably priced Champagne Brunch on the weekend (there is usually a design-your-own omelet station that is perfect for those who like to choose their own fillings).

DeSimones Steakhouse—open Thursday through Sunday from 4:00 p.m. to 10:00 p.m.—offers a premium dining experience with your choice of steak, roast prime rib, delectable beef Wellington or a wonderful lobster bisque. All restaurants have proven to be very accommodating

Railroad Pass Casino entrance. They were just finishing up the parking lot and entrance on our last visit. The new divided highway will take some getting used to, but it makes the ride much more pleasant and it took less time to get there. *Photo by S. Damon, author's collection.*

where dietary restrictions and food preferences are concerned. Quality and taste are constant across the board. If you are staying, you may want to hike the Railroad Tunnels or Railhead and visit Lake Mead and Hemenway Park to get a bit of exercise and take in some gorgeous views of the surrounding area. There are definitely some perfect photo ops.

LAKE LAS VEGAS

The approach to Lake Las Vegas is lovely, with the relatively recent opening of Terrazza Park (2014) at 1992 Galleria Drive, showcasing its roadrunner statues, barbecue pits for family gatherings and beautiful vistas providing a glimpse of what to expect at the lake itself. This is one of the most scenic new parks in Henderson. The entrance to the lake area is breathtaking, with waterfalls, stately residences, greenery and all that sparkling water.

The story of Lake Las Vegas reads like a cautionary tale of what is, what was and what might yet be. The premise was that if you build a 320-acre man-made lake in the desert with two posh, luxurious hotels, a lovely setting crowned by the jewel of the sparkling lake itself, with their vision of a cobblestoned Italian village containing a wide variety of fascinating little shops and restaurants in a resort-like setting, they will come.

The lake was first envisioned by the actor J. Carlton Adair as a project he wanted to name "Lake Adair." He purchased the land and water rights in 1967, but Ronald Boeddeker acquired two thousand acres from the U.S. government after Adair went bankrupt twenty years later. In turn, Transcontinental Properties bought the property in 1990. It took the funds of Co-Chairman Henry Gluck with Texas billionaires Sid Bass and Lee Bass to develop the property in 1995. The lake was built on the Las Vegas Wash, with water diversion beginning in 1990, filled with 3 billion U.S. gallons when completed. Bankruptcy was filed for the massive project in 2008, with debts between $500 million and $1 billion. But by 2010, the project was back in operation after a court battle.

When Lake Las Vegas opened in 2003, people did indeed come—those hungry for the sight and feel of water; those wanting to live on the shore in condominiums; couples desiring to live within the thriving resort setting in luxurious private residences; those planning a wedding at the highly-touted venue; families wanting to spend the day wandering the square, enjoying the slightly cooler air on a hot summer day or tranquil evening; or even those visiting to see the fireworks. Best yet, it is less than a twenty-minute drive from downtown Henderson! The lovely Ritz-Carlton (2003–11), plus the appeal of the Aston MonteLago taste of Tuscany, with its cobblestone streets and fountains, couldn't be resisted. The dining and hotel lodgings at the Ritz were posh and legendary, according to guests who visited in the past. Afternoon tea in the Firenze with tea sandwiches and fresh scones with champagne strawberry jam and

The approach to Lake Las Vegas from Lake Mead Boulevard, heading from Henderson. The waterfalls provide quite a welcome as you get closer to the lake itself. *Photo by S. Damon, author's collection.*

clotted cream were more than memorable. The Medici had all the high-end dining options that connoisseurs of fine dining expect: Fried Buffalo Mozzarella, Roasted Eggplant and Aged Balsamic Vinegar; Dungeness Crab; Asparagus Risotto and Mascarpone Cheese; Rosemary-Grilled Lamb Chops infused with Balsamic Mint Essence and more culinary delights. Club Lounge service provided snacks, appetizers, wine, champagne and desserts. The staff offered personalized service that was second to none. The beautiful Casino MonteLago was a great draw for those who loved to gamble in a comfortable, more intimate setting without having to face the hustle and bustle and the crush of crowds on the Strip. It was smaller, friendly and had live music after 6:00 p.m. on the weekend evenings and great giveaways as comps. Many locals still talk about it once being *the* Henderson casino.

Then the real estate crash and recession happened, foreclosures loomed and the three pristine golf courses were forced to close (one was reopened shortly afterward). Darker days followed in 2011 with the demise of the ever-so-popular Ritz-Carlton. The subsequent 2013 shuttering of the Casino MonteLago, the only casino on property, seemed to sound the death knell. The problem with a place designed solely on luxury is that when a recession hits, folks move out. Walking the cobblestone paths is still a delight, but the closed-down fountains and unkempt areas can't be negated by the lovely lakeside setting.

Quite a few businesses closed as the grounds of MonteLago Village became less appealing and some of the charm went out of the place. This meant that even fewer guests made the trip to the lake or booked rooms at the hotel. Everyone had their favorite places to frequent and simply stopped making the short drive once those establishments closed. The Auld Dubliner was one of the most popular venues in the square. Its Fish 'n' Chips was especially tasty—a large portion of crispy, crunchy fish with fresh-fried chips—but the juicy burgers and crisp fries were also touted as delicious. Its MonteLago Beer Fest was enjoyed by all who attended. It brought new life to the waning lakeside MonteLago Village. And then there was the Auld Dubliner's legendary St. Patrick's Day celebrations featuring Guinness beers and "swag" (as one source put it).

Everyone was sad to see the place close, and they kept hoping for a grand reopening with the return of Renee the server, and it now has (although I don't know if Renee was there). The Auld Dubliner's premises were reopened in March 2018 as The Pub and did resounding business during the Memorial Day weekend. It was good to see it up and running

A view of the lake through a portico on the promenade, across from the wedding shop. Imagine having your wedding photos shot here. *Photo by S. Damon, author's collection.*

A view of the Hilton from the courtyard shows that it's still alive and kicking. With the addition of new businesses at MonteLago Village, tourism is on the rise. *Photo by S. Damon, author's collection.*

The front façade of Le Café du Lac in MonteLago Village is a beautiful little place that is also very pet-friendly. Most of the shops offering treats will give you a little paper cup for your pooch if you ask. Some even have "pet watering" stations outside. That and the misters are a nice touch when it's hot outside. *Photo by S. Damon, author's collection.*

The slightly overgrown Lake Las Vegas courtyard. Only one fountain was operating at the time, and that was because of a nearby photo shoot. It's a sad contrast to a visit back in 2015, although business is picking up in MonteLago Village itself. *Photo by S. Damon, author's collection.*

again since our last visit. The Pub obviously offers traditional pub food with a definitely tasty twist served in a beautifully renovated restaurant and bar with a great view and atmosphere. The appetizers are tasty: tacos, chips, soda bread, sausage rolls and greens. You want delicious prime rib dip or a BBQ chicken sandwich? Got it! How about authentic fish 'n' chips, ribs, curry, meatloaf or a "gourmet pub burger"? And yes, they are continuing the tradition of the MonteLago Village Beer Fest!

Shops on the premises are also showing some revitalization, with signs on the windows and doors promising "Opening Soon," while some new restaurants and interesting pubs have already opened their doors, to the delight of Lake Las Vegas residents and guests. This can only be good for the future of this special site. One of the best features of the premises is that it is and always has been very pet-friendly, so if Fido likes to take a walk and sniff new aromas, you can even get a little paper bowl of water from most of the establishments to quench his thirst. By the way, the misters used to be a nice touch outside the ice cream shop, although they weren't in operation the last time we visited. There are a lot more options on the water if you are into pedal boats, paddle boats and kayaks, as well as flyboards and jetpacks—or so it seemed to us.

Proof Tavern has opened in the MonteLago Village and has brought with it "upscale American cuisine" (as it's described) and some much-needed gaming—on a limited basis—to liven up the courtyard. You can enjoy breakfast, lunch and dinner (a rare treat to have all three meals offered) in the dining room or on the good-sized patio. If you decide to host a special event, you may want to reserve the private dining room on the second floor. There are half-off burger specials on Sunday, and if you intend to visit with children, you can now enjoy the ambiance on the exterior patio (gaming rules prohibit children in the pub itself). You can choose from a wide variety of appetizers from the "Anytime" menu (including edamame with chili and garlic or teriyaki and ginger; the enticing "Dirty Dirty Chips" with a unique blend of ingredients; or crispy pork belly bites with balsamic, bleu cheese and scallions). For other dining options, you can choose from sides ranging from tots (cheesy or plain), sweet potato or truffle fries or onion rings; a variety of soups and salads (you can have your salad wrapped in a tortilla if you would like to make a meal of it); sammies or burgers (with your choice of side); a delicious variety of flatbreads (the Hawaiian and BBQ are highly recommended); and entrées including beer battered fish 'n' chips, ribs and tortellini. And don't forget the delectable, freshly prepared desserts to eat there or take home.

The Auld Dubliner, now closed for business. People are still missing those lobster rolls. *Photo by S. Damon, author's collection.*

Luna Rossa Ristorante has been a favorite dining spot for many guests at Lake Las Vegas for more than five years now. The addition of this authentic Italian pizza restaurant adds credence to the Tuscany Village décor of the courtyard and promenade. Luna Rossa is owned by an Italian family, which accounts for its authenticity, and is also upscale, which accounts for the prices. Dining options include homemade pasta, thin-crust pizza, mesquite-grilled fresh fish, meat and fowl roasted on spits and many delicious desserts. "Le Insulate" (salads) range from mixed baby greens, carrots and tomatoes in balsamic to a wonderful Caesar salad and a unique salmon and potato salad and more. The antipasti are all amazing, prepared as bruschetta, cheese-filled potato dumplings, baked eggplant, calamari, zucchini, clams and mussels, just to name a few. Then, to tempt you further, you can select from pasta dishes that are second to none (all traditional Italian favorites, with a twist or two to spice it up), or perhaps you would prefer a chicken, salmon or veal main course, or lamb, steak or lobster, served with vegetable and potato (or pasta, an additional cost). As if that's not enough, there are also freshly prepared pasta dishes that will make your mouth water (gnocchi, ravioli, manicotti, tortellini, cannelloni and fettuccini). And that's not all, because after all this lovely lusciousness, you have your choice of dessert. Be it a simple dinner for two or a special event like a wedding or business event, Luna Rossa aims to please.

The invaluable Seasons grocery store, lakeside. We don't know what we would do without it. *Photo by S. Damon, author's collection.*

Seasons, the real grocery store and treat shop at Lake Las Vegas, has remained open throughout all the upheaval since it opened in 2016. It is the staple of the lake, offering a variety of frozen treats for guests, snacks, beverages and groceries for those who live here or prepared snacks for picnickers and families who want to spend the day in proximity of the water. It's clean and very well set up—attractive and inviting to enter. It even has a range of natural and non-GMO/organic products. If you visit on a budget, you can have your choice of a full range of products at a far lesser price than at any of the restaurants. This is a booming business during long weekends but is much more sedate during the off season.

Le Café du Lac has opened its doors, taking over the former home of Lobsterman's Restaurant (famous for its outstanding lobster rolls, chowder, delicious coleslaw and outstanding bread that will be sorely missed). This new French café by the lake has been described as a definite step up from the atmosphere of the previous place. Its menu promises to take you on a tasty Gallic tour of all the favorites loved by gourmands—from "Brittanie to Nice." The (gluten-free) buckwheat crepes and "French cidre" are delectable, and the Pan Banga is highly recommended. You can join crepe-making or pastry instruction classes or purchase some of the finest French pastries freshly prepared each morning by their master baker. The outdoor patio is casual and has a splendid view of the lake—especially perfect for dining during its hours of 8:00 a.m. to 3:00 p.m.

Mimi' & Coco' Bistro (on the prior location of Sunset & Vines, which catered to wine gourmands and offered fine dining) opens at noon and remains open for business until 12:00 a.m. during the week and 2:00 a.m. ("or so") on Friday, Saturday and Sunday evenings. This lovely French-themed lakeside restaurant is simply beautiful, with its combination of interior artwork and stunning architecture that enhances the view. The setting couldn't be more perfect for weddings, special events and parties, which are its specialty. The menu is quite extensive, with everything you could desire: a charcuterie board, appetizers (such as Escargots de Bourgogne and calamari), delicious grilled chicken or veggie-friendly sandwiches, main dishes (filet mignon with or without lobster tail and veal Provençal come highly recommended), plus a variety of soups, salads and sides.

The Hilton Lake Las Vegas Resort & Spa is alive and well and as popular as ever after taking up the reins from what was first the Ritz, then the Ravella (2011–13) before becoming the Hilton Lake Las Vegas Resort & Spa (2013). The Firenze Lobby Lounge is touted as an excellent open-air bar and lounge that invites you to try various cocktails from around the world. Snacks are, of course, also available. The Medici Café offers dining "al fresco," with seasonal favorites prepared at its open-air kitchen, with a beautiful view of the Florentine garden. The seasonal Pool Bar & Grille allows you to relax outdoors in the open air or under a cabana while enjoying snacks and drinks. If the pool is closed for the season, you can always order room service. And yes, MonteLago Village and the Hilton are pet-friendly (up to fifty pounds).

Vino del Lago, with its "Summer of Jazz," opened in May 2018 and now features an inviting jazz lounge with some of the best jazz singers

The Mimi' and Coco' Bistro is now open for business—and how lovely it is! *Photo by S. Damon, author's collection.*

in town. Creators Ken and Teri Hutchinson also promised tapas in the lounge, a great addition. The wine dispensary is something totally unique to the lake and is a perfect way to do a tasting—purchase a card, select, dispense and enjoy something different than you may otherwise have ordered from a regular menu. More will be offered as time passes and further arrangements can be made, but what a great start.

Postscript

What Goes Around Comes Around

Fusion of Old and New

Since its inception, Henderson has been a boomtown. In the general span of time, its sixty-five-year history is very short, yet this city has exploded from its tiny core of 13 square miles to its current 108 square miles within that time. The population has expanded to more than 293,000 individuals by current estimations, and it just continues to grow. Businesses open and close—like the tiny but immensely tasty Burger Shoppe, which operated for just three months offering its freshly prepared burgers and fresh, extra-crispy golden fries. Older businesses fold as the original owners are bought out, retire or when economics make it difficult to compete with more lucrative businesses with better financing. Still others like Coo-Coo's and the Gold Mine Tavern thrive by adapting and rolling with the times.

City of Henderson business plaza and downtown Henderson stores, including Bowling, Safeway, Western Auto, Sporting Goods and Fish 'n' Chips, 1964. *City of Henderson Secure Files (copy of original), used with permission, photo #00038.*

Tucky's Smokin' BBQ, at 308 North Boulder, has brought back the flavor of true hickory-smoked meat to town—reminiscent of the old mobile front street BBQ remembered by a few lifelong locals—but in a comfortable, homey, rustic-type setting. The site makes its own pickles, bacon and BBQ sauce and only uses "100% food grade wood from sustainable sources," as the website states, so the flavor is nothing but pure and clean. When the contents of the two or three pits filled with pork, chicken and sausages are gone, that's it! Better luck tomorrow! But it works. You can always see steady business at this out-of-the-way restaurant, and it's good to see a new place really take off. Best yet, there is no pretense, with the rolls of paper towels on the table for those of us who like to be ourselves and immerse our fingers in the pure goodness of real hometown, home-smoked deliciousness. Not inexpensive by any means, it is consistently tasty (especially the brisket and burnt ends).

Some newer coffee shops are still thriving. Sunrise Coffee at 3130 East Sunset Road has been around for several years now, since Juanny Romero and her husband, Joshua, first opened the doors of their establishment in 2008. It offers vegan food and twenty-ounce beverages, perfect for the UNLV crowd. This was followed by the quiet opening of Mothership Coffee Roasters, a specialty coffee experience at 2708 North Green Valley Parkway, in 2015. Mothership has a great reputation for delicious homemade pastries and some of the freshest espresso and coffees to be experienced—from domestic to international. Joshua taught himself the roasting process and how to prepare the perfect espresso so he could make the best brews possible. The shop is small but clean and bright, the clients are loyal and the atmosphere is cozy and friendly. Those serving you know their craft. Since the beginning, this has been a place where folks can drop by and enjoy a hot or cold brew, depending on the season. The variety is impressive and of the finest quality. There is an espresso bar, filtered coffee, cold brew and freshly baked pastries each day. How can you possibly go wrong? Perhaps this is why it is growing in popularity while other places are closing their doors. Besides, let's face it—the name itself is just plain cool.

Bad Owl Coffee, at 10575 South Eastern, is big with college students and other discerning locals. Its Harry-Potter–esque atmosphere and décor make it a fun place to enjoy a freshly brewed java with friends or colleagues. The management has obviously found its niche with a unique flavor all its own. The menu includes espresso, kyoto (traditional Japanese iced coffee), nitrogen-brewed coffee, a variety of lattes and mocha, sparkling beverages, delicious teas, toasts, overnight oats (yes, they are wonderful), sandwiches and waffles, plus yummy pastries. The apple malt tea and butterbeer latte come highly recommended. It is, in a word, magical.

GROWING PAINS AND THE STRUGGLE FOR SURVIVAL

Unfortunately, the planned revitalization of parts of Henderson has been stymied. The Galaxy Theater side of East Sunset Road is mostly booming with the theater, Smith's, Barley's Casino, Olive Garden, TGI Fridays and a variety of other restaurants and successful businesses. On the other side of the street, Trader Joe's and restaurants such as Enzo's Ristorante and Weiss Deli are as popular as ever, as are a few fast-food joints stretching between Green Valley Parkway and West Sunset Road.

Enzo's, situated at 2724 North Green Valley Parkway, has been a neighborhood gathering place since 1987. It originally started in New York in 1979, but then the owner moved the restaurant to Henderson and a New York–flavored pizza legend was born. Its thick crusts and Neopolitan-style pizzas bring in patrons from all over the Valley. Weiss Deli (and Bakery)—almost next door at 2744 North Green Valley Parkway—is a breakfast and deli shop that has been a staple in the East Sunset/Green Valley area for more than twenty years. Its baked goods are always fresh and delicious, and its corned beef or pastrami sandwiches, chicken noodle and matzo ball soup are outstanding. It has salads, delivers and is most definitely a true "Jewish Deli." It is reassuring that despite all the changes in the area and closures of various restaurants, these places continue to thrive.

Sometimes places open and just don't seem to last too long. Either they fall under new management or casino operators decide they want to change things up. Such was the case with the small Gold Rush Casino, located at 1105 West Sunset Road. This was a tiny place that opened in 1998 and closed in 2012 when Station Casinos bought the business and transformed it into the current Wildfire Sunset. There were mixed comments from guests who enjoyed visiting it when it was the Gold Rush. "The $4.00 local breakfast menu and $2.99 for ¼ lb burger with fries or $1.49 breakfast special were a definite draw," recalled a longtime guest who was a frequent patron. Folks loved the fact that it was tiny, with a personal touch and homey feel, but the restaurant area was surrounded by open walls that led to increased noise from the casino and a rather smoky dining atmosphere. Decorating updates and a change of menu have made the Wildfire Sunset a consistently comfortable albeit still intimate place to visit. It's different now because the Wild Grill (café) is best known for offering the opportunity for you to build your own burger with your choice of "bun, protein and toppings." You can even make it a lettuce wrap, as we found on a recent visit. The food is delicious and reasonably priced (with some very tasty options), the service is friendly and on-the-spot and the place is comfortable. We even managed to win a few bucks on the way out. Win/win all the way!

MORE RECENT CLOSURES WITH CHANGING TIMES

In May 2018, celebrity chef Carla Pellegrino, chef and owner of Bratalian Neapolitan Cantina in Henderson, announced her plans to close her restaurant. Between the revenue loss after a car plowed into the front wall in 2016 (resulting in a closure of eight weeks) and the increase in rent, this unique place could no longer afford to stay open. It offered a variety of traditional Neopolitan dishes, including pork/veal/beef meatballs in fresh tomatoes and basil sauce and the very popular spinach and ricotta raviolis. Appetizers included fried calamari and zucchini, Prosciutto and melon and the delicious House Mix Appetizer. Entrées included veal and chicken dishes, sausage and bell peppers, pork chops and salads. Pastas were authentic and delicious. And then there were desserts. She opened the Brazilian/Italian restaurant in 2011, and residents enjoyed the casual dining atmosphere. Her sister, Alessandra Madeira, helped her on a daily basis. There is hope for a new "unique concept," as she put it, to open by fall.

The District @ Green Valley Ranch is also having its own issues with turnovers of businesses. The Due and Proper bar (a British pub with a retro UK design, pub treats and a huge "shots" wheel) and Whist Stove & Spirits gastropub (with its European interior and American-themed fare) had both found comfortable niches at the District @ Green Valley Ranch (GVR) since their opening in 2014. Reviews were good and guests were enthusiastic. These places were such a departure from the original bars that had attracted the working class years ago. Unfortunately, Whist Stove & Spirits and the Due and Proper announced their closures in May 2018. The giant PKWY District has announced that it will be taking over the space. Lyfe Kitchen in Green Valley Ranch closed in April 2018. This "healthy lifestyle" restaurant was a fixture in GVR since 2014. Its motto of "Love Your Food Every Day" introduced diners to food that was tasty and actually good for you, with separate menus for vegans, vegetarians, those on gluten-free diets and those of us who remain "omnivores." The attractive "herb wall" was a feature, showcasing twenty-five popular herbs from the menu. It is being replaced by SkinnyFats, with its healthy or "live happy" menu.

Outback Steakhouse, at 4423 East Sunset Road, was a neighborhood fixture for years. Folks walked there from their apartments as well as arriving by car.

Many people dropped in on their way home from work or had celebrations in its comfy, old-style dining area. It was nestled way back in a parking lot—a strange place for a chain such as this—but then again it was different than any other Outback, and the crowd loved it, keeping the servers hopping and the place packed. Every time we went there, it was doing brisk business, and the food was consistently delicious with very friendly service. Then it was abruptly closed in 2014, as the owners built a new, larger Outback on Stephanie—another ding to an area plagued with closures. Apparently the new location is much more comfortable and inviting, but there was just something special about going into this old favorite and enjoying your meal in a very casual atmosphere. This was one place we really missed after its closure, and our neighbors felt very much the same. You don't often find a reliable restaurant in a convenient location literally right next door.

Joe's Crab Shack at 4250 East Sunset Road was one of many chain locations closed during the summer of 2017. Guests loved the laid-back atmosphere and beach-themed décor—not to mention the crab buckets and other seafood favorites. It has been mentioned by many as a favorite, especially since it's not that easy to find a good, affordable seafood restaurant in this area. The place was always rather busy, populated by loyal patrons, and it was definitely a recognizable local fixture on Sunset Road. Reviews were generally favorable for a family-friendly restaurant, so it came as a bit of a shocker to locals and employees when the parent company decided to give it the axe due to bankruptcy. There is nowhere else in Henderson quite like it, and guests from out of town and folks from other parts of Las Vegas are still looking for it at its old location. There are places that are just part of a chain and places that are specially remembered for offering something otherwise lacking in a community.

BEST INTENTIONS

The Water Street District was planned as a vibrant place to shop, eat and visit once revitalization was complete. Until the middle of 2018, it appeared that the only businesses truly thriving were a few coffee shops, bars and the historic casinos. The addition of several new businesses (including Juan's Flaming Fajitas and Cantina), plus the popularity of such enduring businesses as Chef Fleming's, Sunset Pizzeria and the Rose Garden, has ensured that regulars return, bringing new guests with them. Established shops are hanging on, backed by owners and investors who believe in the popularity and historic value of this area of town. But they also want some guaranteed return for their capital, which means that more residents have to be drawn to this hub. The Country Fresh Farmers' Market—albeit with fewer vendors than originally envisioned—breathes life into this commercial area, offering fresh fruit and vegetables and a few crafts or local honey as well. This cooperative, with its convenient location, draws visitors to the historic part of town, and folks from other parts of Henderson and Las Vegas enjoy the market atmosphere in the desert. At its peak in years past, you could get a great deal on fresh produce, baking, prepackaged food, candy, crafts and other true market items, but over time, the number of vendors has decreased while prices have increased. The city-offered coupons to fixed-income residents do help make it bustle on Thursdays. Driving through downtown Henderson on weekday evenings or an early Sunday morning—and this is one of my favorite places in the city—you can see it's still a bit of a ghost town, with the feel of small-town America where the shutters have been pulled and places have closed down for the night. The popular restaurants and bars such as the Rose Garden and the new Goldmine and casinos like Emerald Isle, the Rainbow Club and the Eldorado (offering breakfast, entertainment or late-night dining) provide some foot and vehicular traffic, but as yet, it's just a promise of what may be. Special events, such as those held at the Events Plaza, offer a much-needed draw and advertising for this wonderful part of our town.

The True Nature of Henderson: Growth, Change and Redevelopment

Henderson was "born in America's defense" ten years before incorporation, during the building of BMI. When President John F. Kennedy visited our town in the beginning of the '60s, he described it as a "city of destiny." The City of Henderson Preservation Plans states in the Mission Statement: "As a battle-born city in a battle-born state, the City of Henderson is a unique place with a unique history. It is necessary to preserve our historic places for future generations, while allowing our city to grow and evolve. To know our city's past is to understand our city's future." Therefore, "The preservation of these important places in Henderson [such as surviving remnants of the BMI site and historic buildings] will provide future generations with tangible evidence of the history and heritage of the city. Historic places portray the unique aesthetic character of a city and serve to educate and be enjoyed by its citizens. Additionally, historic preservation can provide economic benefits for a community through tourism, tax incentives,

The words "Western Gambling" on the sign have replaced the former "Casino Center." The wording suggested by Mrs. E.E. Blanchard of Boulder City won her fifty-five dollars in a contest conducted by the local chamber of commerce. *City of Henderson Secure Files (copy of original), used with permission, photo #00028.*

and adaptive use and rehabilitation." Clark County Museum, at 1830 South Boulder Highway, is also home to carefully rebuilt and restored former residences and businesses that show exactly what life must have been like during Henderson's formative years.

There are glimmers of hope to ensure Henderson's growth and development. The Cadence Master Planned Community—located north and east of Lake Mead Parkway and Boulder Highway in Henderson—consists of 2,200 acres with a 50-acre central park at its heart. Some of this property was previously used for BMI or other industrial purposes and/or a legal dumping ground, so it was contaminated with dangerous amounts of asbestos, pesticides, metals and other materials. According to the planners, they have been working since 1991 to get it cleaned up. In 1992, a subsidiary of Basic Management Inc., the Landwell Company, was created to develop land that had been held by BMI since 1952. In 1999, another subsidiary was created, Basic Remediation Company, LLC, with its sole purpose being to carry out the restoration of the 2,200 acres east of Boulder Highway.

You can see the difference this makes to the Henderson landscape: new schools, stores, businesses (including many new restaurants that have opened or will be opening soon), walking and bike trails, parks to add more spots to Henderson's "green" reputation, thriving new communities and all the markers indicating where future homes and even a new casino will be built. The view from some of the areas—whether of mountains or the Strip—is awesome. It is good to finally see the vast stretch of BMI land being used to benefit our town and bring things full circle, as based on Henderson's original premise—building a city from the ground up and repurposing existing property to better serve the community.

A recent article in the *Review Journal* envisions a new Henderson. According to the article, "City officials have big plans for Henderson. They envision a suburban utopia filled with plenty of open spaces, parks, community gardens and access to all modes of transportation—maybe even a light rail. Restaurants and retail stores will fill downtown. As a first step in their vision, the Henderson City Council adopted Henderson Strong, replacing the city's master plan that was adopted in 2006."

Planners expect a boom in Henderson's population to an additional 100,000 residents within the next twenty years—largely due to the National Football League Raider's new long-term home near the M Casino and also due to our Golden Knights. But, the article continued, "city leaders want more than a healthy economy. Henderson will have more community gardens, grocery stores in food deserts and a mobile farmers market called the Veggie Buck Truck." With all this expansion, Cadence and the new Union Village located just west of Boulder Highway near U.S. 95 and Galleria Drive (incorporating a flagship Henderson Hospital and other perks) can only better serve the city.

Business owners in the downtown area hope that all this positive growth, opportunity for preservation of history and dreams for the future will extend to them. Some residents fear the change to our quiet town, while others celebrate new opportunities and resurgence of the Water Street District with city incentives and a drive to succeed.

Perhaps there truly is a way for experts to balance the restoration of the historic "old" with the excitement of the "new": to reopen old businesses or find investors to purchase and renovate defunct places that are an eyesore and such a waste of prime property to once again make them viable. The fact is that as our town continues to grow and expand, the population continues to increase at a steady rate. After all, Henderson is and always will be, as promised, "A Great Place to Live."

Sources

Bullinger, Dana, Digital Projects Librarian, Henderson Libraries. Files retrieved.

City of Henderson Secure files, used with permission.

City of Henderson, Nevada. CityofHenderson.com.

Facebook. "You Know You're from Henderson if…." https://www.facebook.com/groups/HendersonIf.

Forbes. www.forbes.com.

Henderson Historical Society. Files and conversation.

Henderson Public Library Digital Files. hendersonpubliclibraries.com.

History of Flooding, Clark County, Nevada, 1905–1975. Flood Hazard Analysis Special Report, n.d.

Las Vegas Review Journal.

Las Vegas Sun. Information related to the history of Henderson.

Nevada Public Radio.

NextDoor. "Henderson, Nevada Neighborhoods, Events and More." https://nextdoor.com/city/henderson--nv.

1950 Census of Population, Nevada. Public information found by searching by subject online.

O'Brien, Colleen. City of Henderson City Clerk's Office. Files retrieved.

Oliverra, Toni, the Gold Mine Tavern. Conversations and a detailed phone interview.

Smerek, James "Jimmy." Interview, information related to Basic High School and the growth of Henderson.

Index

D

E

F

G

H

J

K

L

T

V

W

About the Author

Sharon Damon has been writing as long as she could hold a pencil—scribbling poems and reading at age four, writing little stories at age six and publishing her first real book of poetry, *Raindance*, at the ripe old age of forty. During that time, she has dedicated most of her life to raising her children and working with children as a substitute/supply teacher and preschool instructor, as well as being a director, supervisor or enrichment specialist for other educational establishments throughout Henderson and her hometown of Winnipeg, Manitoba, Canada (where she earned her BA, BEd in English, music and early childhood education). Her life experience is broad—baker's assistant, HRA, researcher, music teacher, Brownie leader, creative writing and baking instructor and more—but she always seems to find her way back to the keyboard.

Sharon and her husband, Mike, share a passion for history and a love for their home in the historic Henderson area, which led her to her creation of this book. They have been eating their way through Henderson for more than twelve years now and don't plan to stop any time soon. Sharon and Mike enjoy traveling Nevada with their pup, Charlie. They are confirmed Disney and music aficionados and love their grandchildren! Sharon has researched and written more than one thousand articles for various online publications as an independent writer and journalist and has learned from each experience while honing her craft. Her poetry has also been published in the International Library of Congress numerous times. Like all writers who live for their craft, she has several other books and projects cooking on the back burner.